FIRE
CANOES

FIRE CANOES

Steamboats on Great Canadian Rivers

ANTHONY DALTON

VICTORIA · VANCOUVER · CALGARY

Heritage House Publishing Company Ltd.
heritagehouse.ca

Library and Archives Canada Cataloguing in Publication
Dalton, Anthony, 1940–
     Fire canoes: steamboats on great Canadian rivers / Anthony Dalton.

(Amazing stories)
Includes bibliographical references and index.
Issued also in electronic format.
ISBN 978-1-927051-45-0

     1. River-steamers—Canada—History. 2. Steam-navigation—Canada—History. I. Title. II. Series:
Amazing stories (Victoria, B.C.)

VM461.D35 2012   386'.224360971   C2011-908409-0

Series editor: Lesley Reynolds
Proofreader: Liesbeth Leatherbarrow

Cover photo: The sternwheeler *Whitehorse* passing through Five Fingers Rapids on the Yukon River.
Photographer Claude Tidd, Yukon Archives 8415

The interior of this book was produced on 100% post-consumer recycled paper, processed chlorine free and printed with vegetable-based inks.

Heritage House acknowledges the financial support for its publishing program from the Government of Canada through the Canada Book Fund (CBF), Canada Council for the Arts and the province of British Columbia through the British Columbia Arts Council and the Book Publishing Tax Credit.

16 15 14 13 12 1 2 3 4 5

Printed in Canada

For Steve Crowhurst

*I do not know much about gods; but I think that the river
Is a strong brown god—sullen, untamed and intractable.*

—T.S. Eliot, "The Dry Salvages"

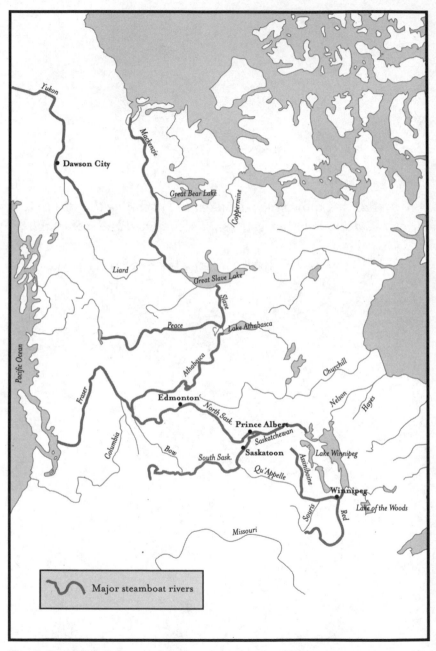

Great Canadian rivers and major steamboat routes. ADAPTED WITH THE
PERMISSION OF NATURAL RESOURCES CANADA, COURTESY OF THE ATLAS OF CANADA

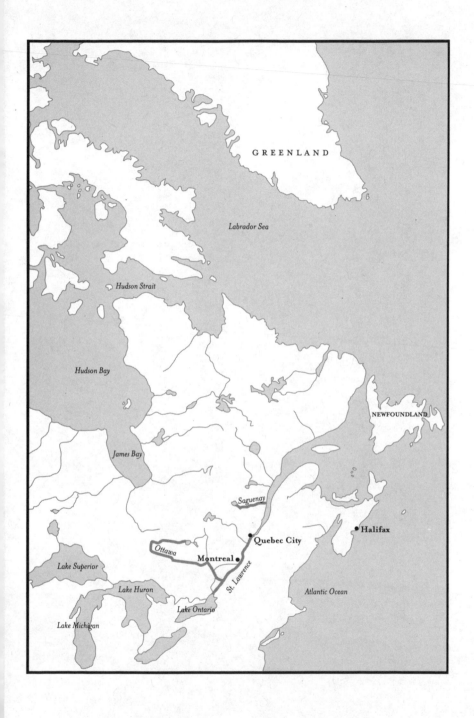

Contents

Prologue

"LET GO FOR'ARD." *The steamboat trembled, ready for release into the main stream of the river. Deckhands retrieved the heavy mooring lines and coiled them on the foredeck. Deep inside the big boat, cordwood was burning fiercely, heating the water in the boiler, which in turn created steam under great pressure to drive the vessel.*

"Let go aft." The final ties with the shore were released. Freed from the constraints of her overnight dock, the stern-wheeler City of Medicine Hat *moved slowly away from the riverside wharf and swung out into the current of the South Saskatchewan River. On the bridge, the owner, Captain Horatio Hamilton Ross, watched without expression on his face as the dirty brown water swirled around his steamboat.*

Only the whitening of his knuckles where his hands clenched the wheel showed his concern.

Captain Ross was suffering from a hangover, as were most of his crew. In the early summer of 1908, Saskatoon was a growing city with a string of bars and brothels sprawled along the banks of a fast-flowing and, at the moment, flooded river. City of Medicine Hat *had spent Saturday night tied up near the southwest edge of town, upriver a short distance from the Grand Trunk Pacific bridge. The captain and crew had enjoyed themselves ashore overnight, but now there was serious work to be done.*

Saskatoon straddles the river, its opposite sides connected by a series of bridges. City of Medicine Hat *was en route to Winnipeg loaded with freight from her home port in southern Alberta. Despite the speed of the river's current, Ross navigated his 130-foot-long boat under the Grand Trunk Pacific bridge without incident. Ahead was the Canadian Northern Railway bridge. With the river in flood, the big sternwheeler couldn't possibly squeeze under its span; there just wasn't enough room. Ross anchored the boat in midstream and sent crewmen to measure the clearance. They reported back that if they lowered the smokestack, or funnel, part way, the boat would just about scrape under the bridge.*

Ross agreed, and as soon as the crew had finished lowering the stack, he hauled anchor and aimed for the middle of the span. The crew had done their work well. The boat slid under, but by only a small margin. Success and failure often went hand in hand, and so it was that day. There was another danger that the crew had not noticed. The Canadian Northern Railway's telegraph wires, which were strung low along the side of the bridge, were now hidden just under the surface of the flooded river. The bow and hull slid over them, but the wires caught on the rudder and sternwheel. They tangled and made the boat impossible to steer. Ahead was yet another bridge, for pedestrian use, and it was obvious that the out-of-control boat would not go under that one.

Captain Ross, almost certainly sober and wide awake by then, did his best to control his charge, but it was an impossible task. He rung down for full astern, but it was too late. The powerful South Saskatchewan River current had the boat in its grasp and would not let go. A courageous crewman risked his life by diving overboard from near the bow with a rope tied to his waist. Swimming hard, he reached the shore, scrambled onto the bank and secured the rope around a sturdy tree. It was a magnificent but futile gesture. Tethered at one end and free at the other, the big boat swung sideways across the current and slammed into the bridge, just as a herd of cattle were being driven over it. Pandemonium followed hard on the heels of the disaster.

Introduction

AS WE PASSED THE ELONGATED expanse of Anticosti Island, the Gulf of St. Lawrence funnelled into the St. Lawrence River estuary. The province of Quebec flanked the river on both sides, and for the first time I experienced the beauty of eastern Canada's vibrant fall colours. Ahead, as the river narrowed and picturesque villages became visible in the soft autumn light of early morning, was the promise of Quebec City. A day beyond that was Montreal and the end of the voyage. I was an excited 17-year-old boy on the foredeck of SS *Empress of Scotland*, a large steamship owned by the Canadian Pacific Steamship Company. I had just crossed the Atlantic from England and was looking at the land that would become my new home.

Introduction

A Canadian Pacific advertisement from that era announced in rather grand fashion, "39% Less Ocean . . . IT'S THE MILLPOND CROSSING . . . only four days—then land in sight, two protecting fingers of Canada lying on either side of the ship, guarding her from ocean tactics. For two unruffled days, your *Empress* glides smoothly up the magnificent St. Lawrence estuary, which narrows to the docks of Quebec City and Montreal."

The last sentence stirs my memories. The St. Lawrence, as I saw it that first time, was magnificent, and the ship did appear to be gliding to its destinations. Far beneath my feet, twin sets of powerful Parsons steam turbines drove the ship forward. High above I could see steam escaping from at least two of the three enormous yellow funnels, each decorated with the company's red-and-white-checked house flag. Crossing an ocean by steamship was exciting. Cruising up a river on an ocean liner between banks that closed in with each passing mile was fascinating. I subsequently cruised up or down the St. Lawrence River at the beginning or end of trans-Atlantic voyages in three other ocean liners: SS *Ryndam*, SS *Ivernia* and SS *Sylvania*. At the time of my initial voyage on that magnificent river, I had no idea that steam had been used to power ships of many sizes on the St. Lawrence and other large Canadian rivers for almost 150 years.

French inventor Denis Papin is credited with designing and building the first functional steam engine in 1690.

His creation was only a model, but it was a good start. He continued experimenting with steam as a motive force for the next 15 years, gradually expanding his knowledge and building increasingly more efficient engines. In 1704, he made a considerable breakthrough when he designed and built a small ship and installed one of his own steam engines on board. It worked. The asthmatic-sounding engine turned a paddlewheel that powered the ship—and the first steamboat was under way.

Other European inventors also were experimenting with steam in the early 18th century. Among a handful of names from that era, that of Englishman James Watt stands out. He created a steam engine for use on rails and so ushered in the railway era. Watt's engine changed the way people travelled on land between cities and towns for generations.

Claude-François-Dorothée, Marquis de Jouffroy d'Abbans, engineered the first practical steamboat, *Palmipede*, in 1776. He sailed the steamer on France's Doubs River. In America, the late 18th century saw similar experiments with steam that changed the concept and style of river travel. As a result, the first steam-powered boats went into operation on the Potomac and Delaware Rivers between 1786 and 1789.

The side-wheel steamer *Accommodation* was the first steam-powered passenger vessel in Canada. Built in Montreal for John Molson (of brewery fame), she began service on the St. Lawrence River in 1809. My voyage up that same river 148 years later took place in the last years of steam-powered ships. Steam, however, had done its job well. It had played an important role in carrying passengers and freight on the greatest Canadian rivers and many big lakes for a century and a half.

The brave and sometimes foolhardy men who ran their riverboats up and down streams and rapids often risked their lives to get the vessels from town to town. In doing so, they left behind exciting tales of flamboyance and daring that coloured the history of Canada; they changed the panorama of our country and affected life in the West, the North, across the prairies and in Ontario and parts of Quebec. These are my favourite stories from the decades when steamboats sent the echoes of their shrill, screaming steam whistles from coast to coast across a vast land of powerful rivers.

1

Anson Northup: An American Entrepreneur

ALTHOUGH JOHN MOLSON'S *ACCOMMODATION* was the first steamboat to work on a Canadian River, credit for the first (and possibly ugliest) steamboat on the long and meandering rivers that cross the Canadian prairies must go to American entrepreneur Anson Northup, a native of Minnesota.

In the mid-1800s, Hudson's Bay Company (HBC) governor Sir George Simpson, ever conscious of saving money for the company, was considering ways of reducing freight costs between Fort Garry and St. Paul, Minnesota. The St. Paul Chamber of Commerce shared Simpson's concerns. As the summer of 1858 drew to a close, the chamber offered a prize of $1,000 to the first person to place a working steamboat on the Red River. In stepped local contractor Anson Northup. He responded to the call but argued for the prize to be increased to $2,000. The chamber's businessmen agreed, and Northup went to work. He purchased an abandoned steamboat called *North Star* somewhere on the Mississippi, where it had been operating under the name of *Governor Ramsey*.

Northup navigated the semi-derelict steamboat up rapids and across lakes to reach the Crow Wing River, where he had it dismantled. A river steamboat contains a large number of parts, and many of them—such as the boilers— are extremely heavy and unwieldy. Northup was not deterred by the enormity of the task he had undertaken. He rounded up teams of horses and oxen, and accompanying drovers, and carried everything on an overland trek of 150 miles through the snows of late winter to the Red River at Lafayette. Once on site and with the boat reassembled, he had carpenters erect a rough wooden shed-like structure over the machinery and steam boiler. With a wheelhouse on top, the boat was ready for service. Northup, exhibiting an excess of hubris, renamed his vessel *Anson Northup*.

Meanwhile another entrepreneur was making his own bid for the lucrative pot. Captain John B. Pond owned a steamboat with the uninspiring name of *Freighter*. Pond planned to take advantage of the spring flooding and use the high level of the Minnesota River to get his boat to the Red. He didn't make it. *Freighter* ran aground en route anyway. Unable to work her free, Pond abandoned her, and there she stayed until she re-entered the Red River's commercial stakes three years later.

That left Anson Northup as the only contender for the prize. On May 19, 1859, he launched his boat and set course upriver, steering for the south, probably as a form of "sea" trial. Northup and his crew steamed the 45 miles upstream to Fort Abercrombie, in what is now North Dakota. Despite the fact that he was going in the wrong direction for a commercial operation, Northup had launched a steamboat on the Red River, and the cash prize was his. On June 6, he and his crew turned north again, bound for Fort Garry, the HBC settlement at the confluence of the Red and Assiniboine Rivers, 500 miles away as the river twisted and turned. They arrived there in noisy splendour on June 10.

Anson Northup was 90 feet long and 22 feet wide with a minimal draft (the amount of hull under water) of only 14 inches. Her foredeck was loaded with cord wood for the engine fires. Even without that encumbrance, she was far from pretty, but she was functional. Her thunderous arrival in sight of Fort Garry on the flooded Red River caused a heady mixture of excitement and consternation among the settlement's inhabitants and certainly upset the HBC officials. It is likely that few people, if anyone, in the Fort Garry area had ever seen or heard a steamboat in action. Certainly the local Cree had not. They were terrified at the sight and sounds of the river monster that swept into their

In 1859, the ugly *Anson Northup* became the first steamboat to operate on prairie rivers. She later served the HBC as *Pioneer*.

A. ROCHESTER FELLOW ENGRAVING, HBC ARCHIVES/ARCHIVES OF MANITOBA P-453

prairie world belching hot sparks and growling in fury. Noted steamboat historian Theodore Barris wrote that the Cree called the monster *"Kuska pahtew oosi"* or "fire canoe."

Despite the initial surprise, the arrival of *Anson Northup* turned the day into one of fun and celebration, a rare treat for Fort Garry's inhabitants. Within minutes of the steamboat's rowdy appearance, the riverside was thronged with wide-eyed Cree, well-dressed ladies and gentlemen and a host of children. They might not have been aware of it at the time, but a new era of travel on the wide-open prairies was about to begin.

After his magnificent and flamboyant entry into Fort Garry, an elated Anson Northup steamed back up the Red River to Fort Abercrombie. As it was the only steamboat operating on the Red River, he anticipated a wealth of freight would be consigned to *Anson Northup*, especially by the HBC; however, he would be disappointed. The all-powerful Company determined to have nothing to do with the upstart American and boycotted his services. Unable to operate without commercial help, Northup sold his steamboat to brothers J.C. and H.C. Burbank for $8,000 and was not heard of again in the steamboat business or on the Red River.

The Burbanks, it must be said, had not been exactly fair in their dealings with Northup. They had made a side arrangement with the HBC, which bankrolled the Burbanks to buy the steamboat and received a 50 percent reduction on all freight charges in return. Protected by the broad scope of the HBC umbrella, *Anson Northup* became *Pioneer* under the command of former Mississippi river-boat captain Edwin C. Bell. Wearing her new name, *Pioneer* belched and thundered her way north again to Fort Garry carrying freight and passengers—just as the unfortunate Anson Northup had planned.

The Red River was not an easy waterway to navigate, even in a shallow-draft vessel. On the eight-day voyage from

Fort Abercrombie, the newly named *Pioneer* regularly ran aground and had to be kedged off, or her rudders ignored the helmsman's instructions and nosed the steamboat into the riverbank. But she reached her destination. For the Burbanks and the HBC, the voyage was an economic success. The ship steamed back to her Minnesota base carrying more freight and passengers.

In Fort Abercrombie for the winter of 1859–60, the box-like vessel had its power plant overhauled, a third deck installed and the old fittings refurbished. She worked on the Red River for the next two seasons until fate intervened. In the spring of 1862, with a sudden and unexpected drop in water levels as the ice broke up, *Pioneer* ran into trouble and was crushed by drifting floes south of Fort Garry. Her remains were left there to rot.

In one dramatic stroke of fate, the Burbanks had lost their main transport. The brothers immediately went in search of a replacement. They found Captain John Pond's old *Freighter*, still where he had left her, aground and deteriorating. Undeterred, they moved her overland to the Red River and refurbished her inside and out. Once she was ready for work, they renamed her *International*. She was much larger and grander than *Pioneer*, being 137 feet long with a beam of 26 feet and, at 42 inches, having a much deeper draft than her predecessor. There is no denying that *International*'s size made her something of a handicap on the Red River. As soon as the water level dropped in the late summer of 1862, she was effectively marooned at Fort Abercrombie. The ongoing American Civil War and difficulties with the Sioux and other indigenous nations kept *International* out of service until 1870. Without her or any replacement vessel, steamship travel on the Red River ceased for the rest of the 1860s.

The HBC's pride suffered a huge blow when Metis leader Louis Riel dislodged the Company's personnel from Fort Garry in the fall of 1869 without shedding blood on either side. Unbeknownst to Riel, his presence and the political wrangling to come would set the stage for a bonanza of steamboating on large prairie rivers. The Burbank brothers' *International* would be in the forefront of that new era.

CHAPTER

2

Peter McArthur's Fleet

PETER MCARTHUR IS CREDITED WITH building the first steamboat in Manitoba in 1872. *Prince Rupert* was a small, double-decked sidewheeler of 30 tons, and McArthur only used her on the Brokenhead River to move lumber to and from his mill, but it was a start.

McArthur was a 29-year-old carpenter working near Portage la Prairie when Louis Riel's Metis forces captured him at Christmas 1869. After he was freed, he fled south to Minnesota. McArthur returned to the Fort Garry area by way of Ottawa in 1870. In the fall of that year, he started logging beside the Brokenhead River, 50 miles northeast of Fort Garry, and he built a mill overlooking the river. McArthur needed a boat to tow log booms to the mill.

He had watched with interest the few steamboats to visit Fort Garry, so he built *Prince Rupert* to take care of his logging requirements.

A few years later, in the spring of 1877, *Prince Rupert* steamed out of Winnipeg (the new name given to Fort Garry in 1873) pushing three flat-topped barges bound for Pratt's Landing on the Assiniboine River, a little south of Portage la Prairie. The barges were weighed down with 120 tons of freight, making it difficult for the steamer's crew to manoeuvre on the multiple bends of the meandering river. In a straight line, the distance is about 50 miles; on the twisted Assiniboine it would be at least twice that distance. It took three weeks, but they managed it nonetheless. Once the barges had been unloaded, the crew took on a new cargo of prairie produce, including 2,000 bushels of wheat, 2,000 bushels of oats and 1,250 sacks of flour. McArthur had expanded his logging and lumber mill business into a transportation company.

McArthur had his second steamer built at Moorhead, Minnesota, over the winter of 1878–79. Named *Marquette*, with twin smokestacks towering over her decks, she was 130 feet in length and drew only 15 inches. That extremely shallow draft gave her the ability to operate even when water levels were way down in late summer. The elegant sternwheeler joined his fleet in April 1879. McArthur's ambitious plan for his latest acquisition was to send her up the Assiniboine as far as Fort Ellice, in what was then called the North-West Territories (now on the border between Manitoba and Saskatchewan), 500 miles away. No steamer had travelled farther up the Assiniboine than Crawford's Landing, a five-day journey. Beyond that was uncharted river that included two miles of rapids and a 20-knot current.

McArthur had had the foresight to hire Captain Jerry Webber, an American with over four decades of steamboating experience. With McArthur by his side, Webber winched his charge up the rapids with great difficulty, but still managed to reach his destination in eight days from Winnipeg. He made the return journey in five days and is said to have run down the two miles of the Assiniboine Rapids in only a few minutes and without problems. *Marquette* had covered 1,000 miles of extremely difficult river at an average speed of 77 miles per day. In the summer of 1881, *Marquette*, under the command of Captain John Scribner Segers, pushed the boundaries of steamboat travel on the Assiniboine even farther when she continued another 150 miles upstream to Fort Pelly and back again in one week. She was the first steamboat to make the arduous journey.

There were no navigation charts or accurate river maps in those days. Like all the other steamboat captains, McArthur and Webber learned the topography of the rivers and lakes in the region by the simple expedient of hitting rocks or sliding onto mudbanks, especially on river bends, and noting the locations of these obstacles.

Except in times of flooding, prairie rivers were shallow,

and a dry season could render them unnavigable, even for steamers with limited draft. *Marquette*'s hull, distinguished by her shallow draft, was different. She was able to work where other steamers would run aground. In one exceptionally dry August, *Marquette* steamed along the Assiniboine by, her captain said, "practically walking on stones from Ellice to Portage [la Prairie]."

McArthur launched his third steamboat, again built at Moorhead, Minnesota, in May 1881. At 200 feet long, she was the largest paddle-steamer yet seen in the Winnipeg region. McArthur named her *North West* and put her to work. She had sleeping berths for 80 passengers and could carry a heavy load of freight. Designed by John Irish, *Marquette*'s designer, she was further distinguished by the addition of a grand piano in the main saloon.

After only four years of service—albeit four rough years—*Prince Rupert*'s career ended in the summer of 1881. She was obsolete by that time so suffered the fate of being condemned and taken apart, though some of her mechanical pieces were almost certainly used for other purposes. As one steamer died, so another went on to greater glory.

By this time, McArthur had become a highly respected Manitoba businessman with land and logging interests, including at least one lumber mill. He also owned three steamers and was a competent skipper. Already a legend among steamboat men of the prairies, he was about to achieve more. In 1881, McArthur joined forces with two other entrepreneurs, William Robinson and C.J. Brydges, to form the North West Navigation Company. On August 2, 1881, Robinson, the driving force behind the event, launched the huge, luxurious side-wheel steamer *Princess* into the Red River. Built to carry 600 passengers on Lake Winnipeg, *Princess* was 154 feet long.

McArthur, the scrawny Scottish entrepreneur, was a strict Presbyterian with a determined character. He abstained from alcohol and frowned on its use by others. By 1882, he was head of inland steam navigation for both the North West Navigation Company and the Winnipeg & Western Transportation Company. That year he eclipsed *North West* by a small margin when he launched the 201-foot-long *Marquis*. She was the largest steamship on the prairie rivers, and there would never be a larger rival. *Marquis* was destined to work on the North Saskatchewan River along with her sister ships *North West*, *Northcote*, *Lily* and *Manitoba*. All five ships sailed under the banner of the Winnipeg & Western Transportation Company, working for the HBC.

Getting five large paddle-steamers from Lake Winnipeg to the Saskatchewan River was a major challenge. Between the big lake and Cedar Lake, at the approaches to the river, there stood a formidable barrier. Grand Rapids stretched four and a half miles between the two lakes. Over its length it dropped 85 feet with an unpleasant fall of three feet in the middle. No one had ever attempted such a feat. Many men would have said it was impossible to take a big steamer up the cataract, but not Peter McArthur. He was made of much sterner material.

Using a combination of winches and manila warps (ropes) as thick as a big man's forearm, the steam power from the boats and his incredible will, McArthur hauled the huge *Marquis* up the rapids to Cedar Lake. It took him and his exhausted team a full 10 days, but he did it without significant damage to the boat. He followed that triumph by taking *Manitoba* up next, without too much trouble, and then *Northcote*. *North West* proved to be more of a problem. After five days of hard work, she was in the final rapid when she got hung up on a rock and was in danger of being lost. The crew of *Northcote* saved the day by running a towline down the rapid to her and hauling her to a calmer setting above the whitewater. McArthur was lauded as having "performed the finest feat of inland navigation ever in North America."

After he left the Winnipeg & Western Transportation Company in 1882, following an argument about shipping liquor on board the company's vessels, McArthur settled on his farm at Westbourne, a few miles up the Whitemud River from the southwest shore of Lake Manitoba. He still had his logging interests and his lumber mills. More important to an old steamboat man, he was looking out at the long length of Lake Manitoba and beyond it to Lake Winnipegosis.

Over the next year, McArthur built two new sawmills, one near his Westbourne farm and the other 120 miles away at Fairford, on the east side of Lake Manitoba in Portage Bay. He had lumber, but he didn't have a boat to transport it. McArthur set to work to remedy that situation. The result was the side-wheel steamer *Saskatchewan*. Built on his Westbourne land in 1883, she was 110 feet long and became a family favourite. McArthur took his wife and six children with him on most trips, in addition to paying passengers. They had a rosewood piano on board, and three of the daughters delighted in singing while their mother played.

The pleasures of roaming Lake Manitoba on board *Saskatchewan* came to an end at the close of the summer season of 1893. The steamer was towing a barge laden with lumber and carrying many bags of sawdust on her own deck. Somehow the barge caught fire as she passed through The Narrows, almost halfway home from Fairford. The barge's flaming cargo spilled into the lake and drifted with the wind until it caught up to *Saskatchewan*. The flames ignited the sawdust, and soon the steamer was ablaze from stem to stern. The crew abandoned ship and watched from a small boat as *Saskatchewan* burned. First went the cabins, saloons and wheelhouse structures, then the decks, until there was nothing left above the waterline. The blackened remnants sank out of sight in less than 15 feet of water near a small island. It was a sad end to a fine steamer and a huge financial setback for McArthur because his mill at Fairford had also burned down that summer.

Despite his losses, McArthur rose like the proverbial

phoenix from the ashes of disaster. He used his remaining money to invest in *Lady Blanche*, an 80-foot-long single-screw-propelled steamer. She was well worn and looked weary, but after McArthur had spruced her up and changed her name to *Isabelle*, she went to work as a big and powerful tug that could tow just about anything on the lakes. McArthur also strayed away from lumber for a while to act as a purchasing agent on Lake Manitoba for a Chicago fish company. He bought an old steamboat named *Victoria* and converted her to a tug. Together they steamed all over the lake buying whitefish for his employers from any and all fishermen.

By 1898, McArthur had had enough of the fish industry and returned to the lumber business. Seeing opportunities farther north, he moved his family from Westbourne to Winnipegosis, on the southwest shore of the lake of the same name. There he built a new sawmill. He wanted *Isabelle* with him to work on the lake, but that meant he had to get her the 30 miles along the too-shallow Waterhen River. McArthur managed it with his customary inventiveness. According to one of his daughters, he "had two empty barges in tow, and these he lashed, one to each side of the tug, to give her more buoyancy. And empty barrels they were carrying were sunk to help raise the tug over sand bars until finally they got the Isabelle through to Lake Winnipegosis."

A year later, McArthur proved his success at getting

Isabelle up the Waterhen was no fluke. He repeated the exercise with the tug *Ida* and, soon after, with the steamer *Iona*. For the next few years, *Isabelle* and *Iona* were kept busy around the clock, towing massive log booms from the north end of the lake to the sawmill at the other end. *Ida* would have been working on a similar schedule because, by this time, McArthur had at least six lumber camps scattered round Lake Winnipegosis.

An incident from that era showed McArthur's acute understanding of the difficulties of navigation on Lake Winnipegosis. A new skipper was taking *Iona* south, with McArthur on board. The skipper, Jack Denby, said he hit almost every rock on his southbound course and then ran the steamer aground a couple of miles short of its home port. Denby worked the boat free and into dock but decided to quit rather than be fired. McArthur's comment to him was, "Jack, my boy, any fool can run a boat aground, but it takes a good man to get one off." Denby kept his job.

Peter McArthur continued to operate his sawmills, logging business and fleet of steamers on Manitoba's lakes into the early 1930s. He was in his nineties when he sold all his businesses, including the last of his aging steamer fleet. McArthur died at the age of 96 in 1936.

3

The Greyhound
of the Saskatchewan

THE STEAMER, WITH TWIN SMOKESTACKS of grey steel belching black smoke and fiery sparks, thundered along the Saskatchewan River, her sternwheel thrashing the water to foam. In the wheelhouse that towered over the topmost of her three decks, the skipper watched every aspect of the river, constantly alert for dangers, hidden and obvious. The steamer was moving fast, running downstream from Prince Albert toward Grand Rapids. Below decks, the stokers, stripped to the waist and glistening with sweat and dust, piled on more wood to keep the fires hot and the steam at full pressure. On the decks, passengers watched the riverbanks speed by, while in the saloon a card game was in progress. Cigar smoke filled the air inside as the aromatic smell of woodsmoke surrounded the vessel. She was the steamer *North West,* the fastest boat on the Saskatchewan River. Because of her speed and the fast passages she made, her crew called her "The Greyhound of the Saskatchewan."

Designed by John Irish and constructed at Moorhead, Minnesota, in 1881 for Peter McArthur's Manitoba fleet, *North West* was the largest sternwheeler yet seen on the prairie rivers. *North West* stretched 200 feet from her stern paddlewheel to her bow. Her cabin deck alone was over 120 feet long, and from the top of her twin smokestacks she stood 60 feet above the river. In addition to upward of 150 tons of freight, she could carry 80 passengers in comfortable berths and was crewed by 10 officers and 12 deckhands. She sported an expensive grand piano, said to have cost $5,000, in one of her stately public rooms and was equipped with two bridal suites. Her route was to be on the ever-changing Saskatchewan and then the North Saskatchewan River between Grand Rapids and Prince Albert and on to Edmonton. On each of her voyages, her Scottish captain, James Sheets, and his crew had to contend with rapids, changing sandbars and an unpredictable navigation channel that moved from year to year.

On her first voyage, *North West* steamed north on the Red River for Winnipeg. She was bound far beyond. Ahead of her stretched more of the Red River, followed by the vast length of Lake Winnipeg and then the rapids. Her owner, Peter McArthur, took her up Grand Rapids with a combination of skill and luck. Once she was above the turbulence and had entered the placid waters of Cedar Lake, *North West* had reached the beginning of her life's work. From Grand Rapids, the steamer chuffed across Cedar Lake to its northwest corner, where a confusing delta of streams and bays mark the mouth of the huge Saskatchewan River.

The Saskatchewan is actually two rivers that originate in the Rocky Mountains and follow independent courses until they meet about 30 miles due east of Prince Albert. The South Saskatchewan leaks out of glaciers astride the border between Alberta and British Columbia. At first, the waters are part of the Bow and Oldman Rivers. Near Grassy Lake, the two rivers join to become the South Saskatchewan. Under that name, it flows across Alberta and Saskatchewan for over 850 miles to meet its northern counterpart.

The North Saskatchewan River trickles down from the Columbia Icefields and the Saskatchewan Glacier. Gathering momentum and size, it runs south for a few miles before turning east. It crosses mid-Alberta, coursing through Edmonton en route to Prince Albert and, a few miles beyond, joins with its sister from the south. The united rivers carve their way past Nipawin and historic Cumberland House to reach Cedar Lake.

North West was crewed by 10 officers and 12 deckhands. Their task was to get the steamer along the Saskatchewan and North Saskatchewan from Grand Rapids to Edmonton and back again as many times as possible in the open-water

The splendid 200-foot-long sternwheeler *North West* was known to her crew as "The Greyhound of the Saskatchewan." In the 1890s, she was the fastest steamer on the North Saskatchewan River route between Edmonton and Grand Rapids.

HBC ARCHIVES/ARCHIVES OF MANITOBA N16890

seasons between spring and fall. In 1882, as the navigation season came to a close, the steamer channel had moved enough to give concern for the following year. Low water from the spring runoff in 1883 compounded the problem a few months later, and the rivers ran shallow. The low water levels failed to deter Captain Sheets and his men. That summer, they carried 196 tons of freight, plus passengers, on *North West* on one voyage from Grand Rapids to Prince Albert, and they did it at speed. Part of the cargo carried on that run was a fully equipped forge.

Although *North West* was fast, considering her great

size, she still needed adequate depths of water under her keel to stay afloat and to keep the stern paddlewheel turning. Getting her through the 1883 navigation season had been a huge challenge. The following year was not much better. Low water flowing over potentially dangerous rocks and unpredictable channels kept the officers and crew busy on each voyage. Like all the other steamboats on the rivers, *North West* suffered hull and stern-wheel damage from rocks on most of her runs. As a result, *North West* spent the winter of 1884–85 and the early spring on the riverbank at Prince Albert undergoing repairs. While she was laid up, her captain, James Sheets, was transferred to take charge of *Northcote*.

Once back in action, *North West* became a troop carrier for a few weeks, working for the Canadian government. She and three other steamers transported soldiers in pursuit of the Cree chiefs Big Bear and Poundmaker, both associated with the Northwest Rebellion. With the short-lived war over in May 1885, *North West* returned to her regular passenger and freight run.

By the 1890s, *North West* was getting old but was still working, mostly for the HBC. There was now no regular captain to guide her along the difficult channels of her home rivers. Instead she was cared for by first mate Joseph Smith, a Metis from Prince Albert. In essence, *North West* had become a tramp steamer out of necessity. She carried whatever freight and passengers were available, for almost any fare. At any given time, her decks could be covered in bundles or bales of farm produce, sacks of coal or occupied by a handful of cattle—anything to make a voyage pay for itself.

After 15 hard seasons on the Saskatchewan, *North West* was one of the few large steamers still in operation. The inexorable advance of the railways had tolled the death knell for commercial river traffic, and time was running out for the once-elegant *North West* too. In 1896, with not enough work on offer, *North West* was put up for sale. No one wanted her. The steamboat era on the Saskatchewan had run its course for the time being, although the early 1900s would see a resurgence, especially in the lumber trade. *North West* was taken to Edmonton and beached at Ross Flats, on a bend of the river. There she stayed, gradually deteriorating, for three years.

The summer of 1899 brought heavy rains to the prairies. The North Saskatchewan River rose 26 feet above its customary mid-August level. *North West*, in the unprotected riverside at Ross Flats, was raised higher and higher by the flood until her moorings parted and she was set free, with no one on board to save her. The river's uncontrollable current carried the aging steamer toward the newly installed foundations of the Low Level Bridge. Theodore Barris told of a teacher who witnessed the event and reported, "There was a wrenching and crushing sound and the boat passed on over the pier seemingly undamaged. Only the upper deck and pilot house were then out of the water."

The central pier, it proved, had torn the bottom out of the once-proud steamer. The engines and boilers dropped through to the riverbed and left a gaping hole in the hull. *North West* was finished. The steamer once known with pride as "The Greyhound of the Saskatchewan" slid beneath the murky brown waters of the river she had travelled so many times and fell to its depths.

4

Steamboats at War on the Prairies

LOUIS RIEL WAS ONE OF THE most charismatic characters in Canadian history in the latter decades of the 19th century. A Metis, Riel was born in the Red River Settlement in 1844. Sent to Montreal at the age of 14, he was fortunate in receiving an excellent education, most of which took place in a Catholic seminary, and also studied law. When he returned to the Red River at the age of 24, he was bilingual in French and English and possibly could speak or understand one or more Native dialects, most probably Michif, the Metis language.

When the Canadian government in Ottawa sent surveyors to the Red River Settlement in 1869, the Metis people became concerned that they would be moved off their lands.

The Metis are people who descend from First Nations mothers and European fathers, usually French, English, Scottish or Irish. The Canadian government, headed by Prime Minister John A. Macdonald, ignored Metis claims that the land they lived on and farmed was theirs by right of generations. They were considered squatters, and their worst fears were about to be realized.

Louis Riel, now known as the founder of Manitoba, became secretary to the newly formed Metis National Committee. On November 2, 1869, the committee forced a stop to the surveying work and seized Fort Garry from the HBC. A few weeks later, on December 23, Louis Riel became leader of the "provisional government" of the Red River Settlement. After executing Thomas Scott for insubordination and rebellion against the provisional government, Louis Riel was a marked man. He crossed into the United States with his family in the summer of 1870 and went to live in Minnesota. He later moved to Montana.

Riel wasn't the only Metis person who was concerned about the future of his people. Gabriel Dumont was a short, stocky man from the area we now know as Saskatoon. He was a hunter of considerable renown, a natural leader and well liked by most people who met him. Dumont and his family lived in a small house on the banks of the North Saskatchewan River. In the spring of 1884, Gabriel and three companions rode 700 miles south to a small Blackfoot Nation settlement in Montana. Their goal was to seek out

Louis Riel and persuade him to assist the people of the Saskatchewan River valley to establish their legal claims. Riel, by then an American citizen, heeded Dumont's call and travelled north to Batoche with his family. At that time, Batoche was the largest Metis settlement in Saskatchewan.

To say that Riel and the Canadian government did not see eye to eye over Metis concerns would be a gross understatement. On March 7th of the following year, Riel, with the backing of Gabriel Dumont, created a provisional government and wrote a 10-point bill of rights for the Metis people. Among the most important of the proposed rights was the declaration "that patents be issued to all half-breed and white settlers who have fairly earned the right of possession on their farms." Whether or not the Canadian government under John A. Macdonald had time to study the document is not clear. Ten days later, when asked if there was any news from Ottawa, the local HBC factor made a comment that the only answer the Metis would get would be in the form of bullets. And so the rebellion began.

Clashes between Metis and police in the spring of 1885 provoked the government into sending an army from Ontario, under General Frederick Middleton, to put down the uprising. As the military buildup continued toward the inevitable Battle of Batoche, three steam-powered riverboats were commandeered by the government for use as troop carriers and war machines. The most famous of those was *Northcote*, formerly owned by Peter McArthur and the HBC.

Northcote was far away in Medicine Hat when hostilities broke out, and ice was still present on parts of the South Saskatchewan River. Undeterred, Captain James Sheets responded to his orders and called for the boilers to be fired in order to get steam up as soon as possible. The moment the engines were ready, he slipped his moorings and headed downstream. Five days later, *Northcote* arrived at Saskatchewan Landing to assist forces led by Colonel Otter. When the big steamer came into sight, 500 militiamen and 200 civilian workers cheered themselves hoarse.

The other two steamers, *Marquis* and *Manitoba*, were closer to the action, near Prince Albert. They were both frozen in by winter ice and found getting away from their moorings somewhat more difficult than had *Northcote*. *Marquis* did get free but immediately required substantial repairs, especially to her rudders and chains. *Manitoba*, a giant of a steamer at 190 feet long and displacing close to 300 tons, was on the bottom of the river after ice had punctured her hull. She was a total loss.

After *Northcote* arrived at Saskatchewan Landing, the steamer spent the next three days ferrying men, horses, carts and equipment across the South Saskatchewan River. While *Northcote* worked, Middleton was 200 miles away near Batoche, waiting for reinforcements and supplies. With the ferrying job over, *Northcote*, towing two barges loaded with the items Middleton needed, carried them to him at all possible speed.

Captain Sheets had planned a four-day run to meet Middleton, but prairie rivers are not that predictable. *Northcote* was overdue when one of Middleton's officers went looking for her in the direction of Saskatchewan Landing. He found *Northcote* and her barges wedged on a sandbar not far from her destination. Getting the boat and the barges afloat again took massive effort from all on board, which had to be repeated time after time as the vessels kept running aground. Instead of joining Middleton in late April, it was May 5 before they met.

On May 8, Middleton advised Captain Streets that he wanted *Northcote* to be converted into a gunboat. The conversion was simple, but less than effective for the protection of those on board. Thin wooden planking, sacks of oats and bales of hay became the boat's protection, aided by 35 riflemen. The two barges, no longer under tow, were lashed on either side of the boat, reducing her manoeuvrability.

Northcote reached the last river bend before Batoche at about 8:00 A.M. on May 9. The first enemy bullets punched through the wooden planking minutes later. A reporter on board the sternwheeler wrote, "This first shot was evidently a signal to the rebels of the boat's approach, and as she rounded the bend a moment later, she was raked fore and aft with a storm of bullets coming from either bank."

Gabriel Dumont was on the riverbank on horseback. He rode back and forth yelling orders to Metis gunmen, in full view of the riflemen on *Northcote*. Middleton had miscalculated. He and his force were still four miles away when *Northcote* came under attack. As the large boat approached a ferry crossing where a steel cable spanned the river from bank to bank, men on one side lowered the cable in an attempt to capture the boat. They weren't successful, but they did manage to snag the smokestacks, whistle, spars and masts and tear them loose. When they fell on the upper deck, the overheated smokestacks came close to setting the boat on fire. And Captain Sheets had additional worries. Two large boulders shared his stretch of river, and he was in grave danger of ramming them. In an inspired bit of river-craft, Sheets let the current turn the boat and clumsy barges and drifted downstream backwards. His crew looked after the boat and barges while the soldiers kept up a concentrated volley of fire at the Metis army. *Northcote* drifted another five miles until she was out of range and could be anchored in safety.

Four other steamboats—*North West, Marquis, Baroness* and *Alberta*—took on the role of troop transports on the North Saskatchewan, and the rebellion was soon over. *Alberta* ended the brief war by transporting a complete field hospital of wounded, doctors and nurses and their medical and food supplies to Grand Rapids for onward shipment to Winnipeg by another steamer. She would have been an impressive sight as she left, surrounded by a cluster of four laden barges, one of them loaded with the bleeding casualties of the war.

The charismatic Metis leader Louis Riel was executed for treason after a brief trial in Regina following the Battle of Batoche.

Louis Riel surrendered to Middleton's forces three days after Batoche fell. He and many wounded prisoners were taken to Saskatoon on the steamer *Northcote*. Riel was later taken overland to Regina where he stood trial for treason. He was found guilty and sentenced to death by hanging. His execution took place in Regina on November 16, 1885.

Gabriel Dumont outlived his friend Riel by 21 years. During that time, he continued to campaign for Metis rights in Canada.

5

The Red River Flood of 1897

ONE OF THE MAIN NAVIGATION problems encountered on prairie rivers was shallow water. During some spring seasons, that changed for a few weeks when the Red River, among others, flooded the surrounding land. It was not unheard of for the occasional skipper to take a shortcut overland during floods to save time.

The Red River flows out of the flatlands of Minnesota and moves at a walking pace toward the north, where it eventually empties into Lake Winnipeg. On its journey, it collects many smaller rivers, adding their waters to its own. Due to the low-lying nature of the land on either side, the Red River frequently overflows its banks in the spring. In 1861, the flood waters extended for 300 miles, the length and breadth of the Red River valley from Big Stone Lake to Winnipeg. Thirty-six years later, another Red River flood, also of catastrophic proportions, entered the history books.

The winter of 1896–97 was one of the worst in many years. Heavy snowfalls blanketed the land for miles on both sides of the Red River in North Dakota. Old-timers looked at the snow, which was over two feet deeper than the snow that had triggered a flood in 1861, and predicted a spring flood. They were right. On March 31, 1897, the river level at Wahpeton, south of Fargo, stood almost three feet higher than its 1893 level. The following day, flood waters covered the railway line between Wahpeton and Fargo, bringing traffic to a halt. On April 2, the Buffalo River, which flows into the Red, spilled over its banks and created a large lake from Glyndon to Moorhead, a straight-line distance of over 20 miles. The Wild Rice and Sheyenne Rivers also spilled over, and their waters met on April 8. By then, Fargo was already flooded.

Downstream, the real trouble started on April 9. Grand Forks, North Dakota, was staring at a possible disaster. Ice jammed the Red River, but heavy rain farther south was threatening to force the river far above its normal seasonal level. If that happened, towns and farmlands downstream, all the way into Manitoba, would be threatened. A few days later, the river was running high and wild. Storms swept over the region, sending freezing rain to add more water to the building flood.

At Pembina, North Dakota, the city fathers showed their concern for the town and its inhabitants by asking Washington for assistance. The response was quick. Within days, Pembina's citizens were greeted by the sight of SS *City of Grand Forks* steaming up their main street to deliver supplies and take on needy passengers. After a fast run back to Grand Forks, the steamer returned three days later. Captain J. Elton commented on the situation: "The low-lying district from the Snake River to Pembina is appalling. It is one vast sea of desolation, wreck and ruin. In some cases the steamer was as much as two miles from the river channel. Barbed wire fences interfered materially with navigation across the prairies but some thirty families were supplied with provisions. Their homes were out on the prairie and unprepared residents were not used to floods."

In Winnipeg, the Manitoba government responded to the growing emergency on their side of the border by chartering the 92-foot-long sternwheeler *Assiniboine* to steam up the Red River to Emerson and rescue the residents, if it became necessary. With the river rising higher by the hour, the waiting *Assiniboine* was called into service. Under the command of Captain E. Connell, she left Winnipeg on April 22. The captain promised, "I am prepared to take this boat anywhere in two feet of water and am allowed to carry 150 passengers; 500 in case of emergency."

As *Assiniboine* steamed upriver, a reporter on board noted "houses surrounded by water, at various stages of submersion. Some had water up to their eaves, some with only a small portion of the roof visible." Chickens, pigs and cattle sought and found any building or prominence that offered a way to get above the waters.

Emerson sits beside the Red River, just north of the US-Canada border. On April 24, the out-of-control Red River flooded the town. As the river moved north, it spread out to cover the surrounding farms. A farmer from the Manitoba community of Morris described its onslaught: "We saw what appeared to be a cloud on the southern horizon. Then rivulets flowed across the fields, and, to our astonishment, before ten hours had passed, we were in the middle of a lake."

At Morris, those on board *Assiniboine* reported nothing but water as far as they could see in any direction. Emerson was little better off. When the steamer was a couple of miles from town, the mayor and a few others went out to meet her in a small boat and climbed on board. Whether or not Captain Connell was actually following the by-now invisible river's course is not known. It didn't really matter. The water was deep enough throughout the town even for a boat as big as *Assiniboine*. Connell surprised one resident leaning out of a second-floor apartment by shaking his hand as he cruised past, steaming right up the main street and tying up outside a large building in the middle of town. Other residents in and on the buildings and seated in small boats gave the steamer a rousing welcome.

Captain Connell acknowledged their cheers with a smile and accepted those who wanted to get aboard the rescue boat. After a few hours distributing relief supplies, he steered *Assiniboine* to another part of town to load a cargo of endangered horses. That night, on the return voyage, *Assiniboine* moored at Letellier. Another storm was brewing, and the waters were getting rough. By the time she reached Morris again the following day, a full gale was sweeping across the flooded land. Although Connell would have preferred to eliminate the many bends in the river and steam cross-country to save time, the threat of fences and other underwater obstructions kept him to the river's natural route, as far as he could see it.

The gale threw up waves to break over the low bow of the steamer, coating the decks and superstructure with ice. Passengers covered themselves in blankets and stayed as close to the boilers and wood stoves as possible. The dreadful weather did not deter Captain Connell from his purpose. Wherever humans or livestock were threatened, he stopped and took them on board his already overcrowded vessel.

Assiniboine completed her rescue mission and returned to dock in Winnipeg in the early afternoon of April 28. The shallow-draft sternwheeler had proved that prairie steamboats could do a lot more than cruise up and down rivers and rapids with passengers and freight. They could be lifesavers, too.

6

One Man's Disasters: Tales of Captain Horatio Hamilton Ross

THERE IS A STAINED-GLASS WINDOW in Christ Church at The Pas. It is dedicated to an icon of the prairie steamboat era: a man who was loved by the people of the region and who was, without doubt, one of its most interesting and entertaining characters. The inscription below the window reads:

> To the Memory of
> Captain Horatio Hamilton Ross
> of Rossie Castle, Scotland.
> Who Died in The Pas, February 11, 1925.
> A Tribute from His Many Friends.

Born in 1869, Captain Horatio Hamilton Ross, a member of Scotland's gentry, was a world traveller and a man not afraid to take risks. He was wealthy and articulate and possessed both a wild streak and an associated love of adventure. According to Ross, after leaving his comfortable Scottish home as a young man, he went to sea, working his passage round the Horn to San Francisco on a square-rigged sailing ship. From there, he drove north in a covered wagon to the Canadian Rockies and kept himself busy with an eclectic variety of jobs. It is an interesting history, although unlikely to hold much truth. At that time, many members of the Ross family had business interests in Alberta, particularly in the polo world. It is more probable that Horatio left Britain as a young man to join his relatives. In that case, he would have travelled directly across the Atlantic to an east-coast port and then overland to Alberta.

We do know that he became, in no particular order, a cowboy, rancher, gold investor and hotelier. Ross also developed a passion for boats. In the early 20th century, he built or owned eight steamboats of varying sizes on Canada's prairie rivers—and managed to wreck a few of them. He was rarely, if ever, short of money, and it is possible that his parents, Sir Charles and Lady Ross, funded some of his adventures. On arrival in Alberta, he built a grand home in the Canadian Rockies. With studied understatement, he called it "The Lodge."

Ross was restless and unpredictable. Not content with life in his new Alberta home, despite the comforts inside and the spectacular scenery all around, he moved on. Ross arrived in Medicine Hat from Calgary in June 1895. He was a stocky, scruffy individual travelling on the river in a nondescript launch. According to reports, he was planning on continuing down the Bow and South Saskatchewan Rivers to Winnipeg, but something about Medicine Hat struck his fancy, and he decided to stay awhile.

Ross's first venture in Medicine Hat was to spend $30,000 to build a hotel in the centre of town. That edifice became the social centre of the community for Ross and his business friends and their families. His attention span, however, was rather limited. After a few years of high living, he tired of life as a hotelier and decided to become a boat owner and sailor. He was ready to embark on a series of wild nautical adventures, though on Canadian rivers instead of the world's oceans.

Ross constructed a 70-foot-long sternwheeler, which he named SS *Assiniboia*, in 1903, initially for use as a freighter on the South Saskatchewan River. There was nothing exciting about the venture, and it was not a commercial success. Horatio Ross, however, was at his best when entertaining fellow citizens. Perhaps to compensate for the lack of freight business, he introduced tourist-style excursions on the river. As an economic venture, these day trips were a waste of effort, but they were a social triumph and provided Ross and the residents of Medicine Hat with a lot of fun. There was much more partying than work.

The popularity of the day trips prompted a much more ambitious project. In the fall of 1906, Ross and an unknown number of passengers set off on an ill-timed cruise to Winnipeg. Winter comes early to the prairies, and Winnipeg was far away. *Assiniboia* acquitted herself well, reaching as far east as Cedar Lake, Manitoba, an impressive voyage of about 1,000 miles across Alberta, Saskatchewan and part of Manitoba. There, with winter coming on fast, *Assiniboia* ran up on a sandbar and could not be dislodged. Ross decided to abandon the boat for the winter. He paid a couple of local Cree to guard *Assiniboia* until he returned. He then shipped himself and his passengers off to still-distant Winnipeg by a combination of dog team and rail.

Winnipeg in early winter was obviously not to Ross's liking. He didn't stay long before heading off to Egypt to spend the winter in the sun. Meanwhile the two stalwart Cree kept their side of the bargain. While Ross relaxed in the heat of Cairo, they stayed with *Assiniboia* throughout the winter, even as the ice on the lake thickened, surrounded the boat and held her fast, and the snows covered her in a shapeless blanket of white. When Ross reached Cedar Lake again in the spring, he found little left of *Assiniboia* except the engine machinery and two steam boilers. The rest had been splintered by the ravages of winter ice and carried off by the spring melt. The two Cree were still guarding the half-buried remains, just as they had agreed. Ross paid them for their dedication and went off in search of new adventures.

Ross was nothing if not resilient. He travelled back to Medicine Hat and started again. First he sold the hotel, then he commissioned a new and bigger steamboat. Residents with nothing better to do watched in wonder as the skeletal wooden frame of the sternwheeler *City of Medicine Hat* took shape on the shores of the South Saskatchewan River. When completed, she was 130 feet long and 30 feet across her beam. Once her two decks were installed and the smokestack raised, she towered above the surrounding landscape.

Launched with much fanfare in early June 1907, the new sternwheeler was used commercially during the day, hauling passengers and freight on short distances to and from Medicine Hat. In the evenings, she was Ross's party boat, and he entertained his friends on board as often as possible. Making short runs with his steamboat did not fulfill Ross's restless urges in any way; it just helped him pay for the boat. He wanted to do much more with her. He wanted to go travelling. He wanted to keep exploring the great rivers.

In June 1908, Ross loaded the sternwheeler with as much freight as he could negotiate, most notably a heavy cargo of flour, and set off for Winnipeg again. He made it as far as Saskatoon, and there the ambitious plan started to fall apart. His most memorable disaster was about to take place. The South Saskatchewan River is close to 300 yards wide from bank to bank, and it was in flood when *City of Medicine Hat* arrived. Powered by a strong current and at a higher level than normal, it should have given Ross and his crew serious navigational concerns.

Saskatoon was a boom town in those early years of the 20th century. With economic success came the inevitable bars and brothels, many of them lined up along the river's banks. Ross slowed his charge, the sternwheel thrashing in reverse, and eased her to a mooring against the shoreline. He and his crew then spent the night carousing in the bars and possibly sampling the wares in the brothels. They woke up at daylight with hangovers and sore heads, facing a difficult job that required all their faculties to be alert. Hungover or not, they had to take their large steamboat down a racing river that sported a series of low bridges spanning its width. They could have waited and rested until their heads cleared, but that was not Ross's way. He had a cargo to deliver to Winnipeg that took priority over everything else.

As the sternwheeler moved away from the riverbank, the current caught her. Captain Ross got her under control, held her on course and steered her under the first bridge in safety, but he balked at the sight of the second. Anchoring in midstream to hold the boat steady in the swift current, he sent crew members to measure the vertical distance between the river and the underside of the bridge. They ascertained that there was almost enough room, but not quite. They had to find a way to reduce the profile of the smokestack, and that meant lowering it at least partway.

The crew soon solved that simple engineering problem. With the smokestack now at an acute fore and aft angle, Ross had his men haul the anchor, and he steered for the centre of the bridge's span, where the distance between water and bridge was greatest. The bow coursed through the water and under the bridge. As it passed the structure, it slid over CNR telegraph wires that had been slung too low along the bridge's length from one side of the river to the other. The smooth hull passed over the wires too, but the rudder was a different matter. It projected down lower than the deepest part of the hull. Knifing through the water, the rudder and sternwheel collected the wires, wrapped them around each other and tore them from the bridge. In seconds, the boat was out of control and heading for disaster.

Up ahead was a pedestrian bridge, even lower to the water than the one they had just negotiated. There was no way the big steamer could pass under it without tearing off major parts of her superstructure. Unable to steer with the wires wrapped around the rudder, Ross rang down for full speed astern. It didn't help. The river's current was too strong and the boat too close to the bridge. A crewman grabbed a rope, made it fast to a point near the bow, tied the other end around his waist and launched himself into the water. With powerful strokes he succeeded in gaining the shore and tied the rope off to a convenient tree. The action almost had the desired effect—almost, but not quite. *City of Medicine Hat* was too close to the bridge, and as the rope tightened, she swung in an arc. The stern passed the bow and the full weight of the boat crashed sideways into the bridge.

The oft-quoted Murphy's Law states that whatever can go wrong will go wrong. That Sunday morning in Saskatoon was no exception. The big sternwheeler turned broadside across the current and rammed the bridge just as a handful of men and boys began herding a large number of cattle across. The cattle stampeded. The men and boys ran for their lives to avoid the cattle's hooves and the boat that was about to wreck itself on the bridge. On board *City of Medicine Hat*, there was chaos of a different kind. As the boat tried to climb up onto the pedestrian bridge, she listed a full 75 degrees. All the crew, except the engineer, jumped or climbed onto the bridge to escape the endangered boat. The engineer took to the water and swam ashore.

There was no saving the steamboat or her perishable cargo of flour. The boat remained where she had struck, held tight to the bridge by the current. She was there for one year and three days, attacked by the river day and night, until Saskatoon engineers were able to pull her free and allow her to drift away to let the river complete her demolition.

Once again, Horatio Ross proved his resilience and his exceptional response to disaster. He went to Ottawa to claim restitution for his loss, arguing that the government should not have built a bridge of that nature over a navigable river. He wasn't overly successful in squeezing any money out of the government, but he did attend many parties, met a host of influential people and had fun. He also left Ottawa with an unexpected job.

As the newly appointed fisheries inspector at The Pas, Ross decided he needed a new steamboat in which he could perform his latest duties. Accordingly, he went to Collingwood, Ontario, on the shores of Georgian Bay, and purchased a 47-foot-long steam-powered screw-driven tug for $5,000. Harking back to his river cruises on the South Saskatchewan River with the now-wrecked *City of Medicine Hat*, Ross sponsored an inaugural cruise in his newest love. The tug, named *Sam Brisbin*, played host to local dignitaries and citizens on a champagne voyage in sight of the town. The only low point was when a misguided guest or crew member dropped the anchor overboard while the tug was at speed. *Sam Brisbin* stopped so suddenly that four men were pitched off the bow into the bay, Ross among them.

Sam Brisbin was said to be a work of art, in the words of one admirer, "a sweet little craft." Unusual for the times, the boat was fitted with its own telephone system and contained considerable brass, all kept in shiny order by the crew.

Two years later, Ross was back in Collingwood to oversee the launching of his next tug. *Le Pas*, with her Scottish owner at the helm, cruised north and west through two of the Great Lakes, Huron and Superior, and after being hauled

Captain Horatio Ross's steam tug *O'Hell* approaching the dock at The Pas. The tug in the background is Ross's *Sam Brisbin*.
ARCHIVES OF MANITOBA N18521

overland part of the way, joined *Sam Brisbin* at Ross's head-quarters at The Pas. The two tugs were kept busy hauling freight to and from local ports. Ross, however, still enjoyed a good party, and he liked to hold his parties on boats. When his senior employee heard the boss was planning another lively excursion on the water, he pointed out that both boats were too busy to be diverted for a party. Ross's response was typical. "Oh Hell," he is reported to have replied. "I'll just have to go buy another boat." And so he did. Ross went downriver and he found another screw-driven steam tug. Later that same day, he arrived back at his docks and announced that the latest addition to the fleet was called

O'Hell. He had another work boat, and he had his party boat after all.

By this time, the prairie playboy was the owner of Ross Navigation Company. Ross continued to throw parties on his boats, but the company was a serious business venture that made money. Over the next few years, Ross's fleet expanded to include two more screw-driven tugs, *Minasin* and *Notin*. Both had Native captains and crews. Ross was a hard taskmaster, yet from all reports he was a fair one. He worked his crews around the clock when necessary, but he was always ready to include them in his fun times, most notably his wild parties, and he dressed them well. The hard-working members of Ross Navigation wore white uniforms on many occasions, as did their boss.

With business coming in from all directions, two more boats were added to the fleet: *Tobin* and the sternwheeler *Nipawin*, which became the flagship of the Ross Navigation Company. By that time, the steamboat company was the most important operator on rivers and lakes in Manitoba.

After many years of taking great risks on big rivers, Horatio Hamilton Ross, a man who admitted to being afraid of loaded guns, died suddenly, violently and much too young at the age of 55. He accidentally shot himself while he was cleaning a rifle in his office overlooking the Pasquia River at The Pas. With his passing, the prairie rivers lost an effervescent character and a great champion of the steamboat era.

Ross Navigation's flagship, the sternwheeler *Nipawin*, steaming in calm conditions on the Saskatchewan River at The Pas.
ARCHIVES OF MANITOBA N18516

In an equally sad footnote for steamboat buffs, the lovely *Sam Brisbin* was last seen in 1930. In 1944, A.J. Dalrymple wrote in *The Beaver*, "I saw her lying ashore two miles east of The Pas." It is said she was later broken up for firewood. *Le Pas* suffered a similar fate. She was used as a sturgeon-fishing boat for a while but ended her life as a hulk on shore.

CHAPTER

7

Problems on the Saskatchewan Rivers

THE NORTH AND SOUTH SASKATCHEWAN RIVERS are notable for their shallow depths, the number of boulders that litter their beds, dozens of sets of rapids, constantly changing sandbars and snags (half-submerged trees). The rivers are susceptible to the extreme contrasts of flooding in the spring and drying out by late summer. In winter, they freeze over for most of their long distances. Even though the two rivers join east of Prince Albert to become the Saskatchewan River, the bigger river continues to be shallow and subject to natural obstructions.

Navigating large and often heavily laden steamboats along these rivers in the open-water season was a challenge to the nautical abilities and ingenuity of the riverboat men who crewed them. Sometimes the passengers had to join the crews on land and help push, drag or warp the big boats to deeper water. One steam engineer commented on the vagaries of the big river: "That was the trouble with the Saskatchewan; the bottom was too near the top . . . One month I stood on sand at the water level; the same fall there was about nineteen feet of water there."

The Saskatchewan flows out of the western prairies into the northwest corner of Cedar Lake. Diagonally across the lake is the final stretch of the river before it meets Lake Winnipeg. That stretch is called Grand Rapids, and it is the most difficult part of the great river system.

The four and a half miles of the Grand Rapids in Manitoba was a major obstacle to all steamboats. The cataracts start with a mess of whitewater and fall over 80 feet from top to bottom, and they have a distinctive three-foot drop halfway down. This barrier separates the southeast end of Cedar Lake from the northwest corner of the much larger Lake Winnipeg. Getting sternwheelers up the rapids was a serious engineering problem, but it could be done. Peter McArthur had proved that in 1882 when he and his team manhandled four boats up from Lake Winnipeg to Cedar Lake. Some steamboaters ran down its rocky course in safety; some didn't.

The stalwart *Alberta*, built in 1904 for Rufus Mosher & Fred W. Coates and a veteran of the Saskatchewan River, was sold to the Winnipeg Navigation Company in the spring of

1908. On June 6 of that year, with Captain Levi Bellefeuille on the bridge and two experienced Saskatchewan River pilots by his side, the sternwheeler *Alberta* bumped and ground down the watery staircase in about half an hour. One observer described his impressions of the scene: "A procession of hungry, jagged rocks, everyone of which had horns, tusks and a complete set of double-teeth, upper and lower, passed by the boat with horrid rapidity." *Alberta*'s noisy progress over the rocks ripped a hole in her bottom, 6 inches wide by 18 inches long. She promptly sank at the end of the rapids. That would have been the end of most steamboats, but not *Alberta*; she had been built with safety in mind. Her hull had been constructed with 12 watertight compartments along its length.

Nine days after the painful, rugged descent, *Alberta*'s crew had patched the hole and she was refloated. She leaked like a sieve but was able to steam close to shore down the long lake into the Red River and reached Winnipeg without further incident. *Alberta* had just completed a river and lake voyage of over 1,000 difficult miles, and for most of that distance she had a barge lashed to either side of her hull. Having survived the rapids, she was in regular use in the open-water season for the next eight years until she was caught in flood waters at Lockport, Manitoba, and wrecked.

Victoria Rapids span the North Saskatchewan about 60 miles east of Edmonton. It was said that the roar of the rapids was a never-ending feature of the nearby settlement and HBC post at Victoria. Although frequent attempts were made to clear the rapids of insurmountable obstacles, including removing boulders weighing as much as five tons, no permanent safe navigation channel could be marked. The dangers of the rapids were acute and well known. That knowledge didn't stop steamboat skippers from doing their jobs. The steamboats had to go up and down Victoria Rapids and, with many trials and more than a few errors, most of them made it.

Cole's Falls, also on the North Saskatchewan, created its own navigation problems a few miles west of the junction with the river's southern sister. The cataract at Cole's Falls was notorious for the rocks strewn along its length. At times of low water, the rapids became impossible for steamers to ascend or descend. In 1883, Peter McArthur's *Marquis* had to unload cargo destined for Prince Albert at the foot of the falls and return downriver.

When there was enough water at Cole's Falls, captains and pilots climbed their boats up stern first and under full steam, with the paddlewheel thrashing the water into foam. If the steamer lost way and had to go back down, she could do so in relative safety without having to be turned round, a potentially deadly manoeuvre on big rapids. In the opposite direction, running down the rapids, the steamers went bow first with the sternwheel thrashing in reverse to slow the vessel as much as possible. It was nerve-wracking work but always invigorating.

Joseph Soles, who worked on the steamer *Saskatchewan* for a while, told of that steamer's route down Cole's Falls: "We'd go down so far on the south side and then we tacked across to the other side to get out of the big rocks and white water, to get over to the black water to go through on . . . you had to think quick and act quick."

Tobin Rapids, another classic hazard to navigation, was distinguished by mammoth boulders. Each of the other sets of rapids on the Saskatchewans had its idiosyncrasies and its own peculiar dangers.

Steel cables across the river, used to haul local ferries back and forth, were another trial for all steamboat crews. According to one steamboat skipper, they were "an invention of the devil, second only in malignancy to a bridge." The correct procedure when confronted by a ferry cable was for the steamer to sound her whistle. At that warning, the custodian of the ferry cable was supposed to lower the strand into the river, but it didn't always work out that way.

Early in *Alberta*'s long June 1908 voyage from Prince Albert to Winnipeg, she encountered a barrier: a ferry cable strung between towers on opposite banks stretched across the river at wheelhouse height. Captain Bellefeuille called for full astern to keep *Alberta* upriver from the hazard and blew his steam whistle to alert the custodian of the ferry cable. There was no answer. After a few more noisy signals, angry crew members went ashore and, according to newspaper reporter J.S. Evans, "[they] laid violent hands on this arrangement." By that we can assume they cut the cable free of one tower and let it sink. If it was the only way to continue the voyage without delay, drastic measures had to be taken.

Despite the natural and man-made hazards that littered their lengths, the North and South Saskatchewan Rivers were important commercial waterways. The steamboats that served their settlements didn't always arrive on time, but their skippers and crews made every effort to find ways to reach their destinations against any and all odds.

8

Tramp Steamers on the Prairies

APART FROM THE BIG PASSENGER and freight-carrying steamers serving regular routes on the largest rivers and lakes of the prairies, there were dozens of much smaller steamboats plying their trade in the same region. Those tough little steamers would carry anything and everything wherever there was enough water to keep them afloat. They would push and pull heavy barges and drag ungainly log booms in all weather. Among the owners and skippers of those tramp steamers were some unforgettable characters.

Red-haired Captain Richard Deacon ran a flotilla of small steamboats on the North Saskatchewan River between 1890 and the early 1900s. His side-wheel tugs pushed and pulled log booms from the edges of forests to the mills. They hauled tons of gravel, bricks and cement, and they delivered groceries and other goods. On board to run the boats would be a captain and a deckhand—no one else. They did all the work between them.

For a tramp-steamer owner-captain like Deacon, time was everything. Pick up a load of freight at one location, steam hard to another and deliver it. Then start again. And nothing stopped the fiery little Englishman from getting to his destination. On one journey carrying a cargo of bacon to Prince Albert, he ran out of cordwood. Determined to complete the voyage, he yelled at his crew, "Fire in the bacon."

When navigation became impossible due to low water levels, Deacon waded along the river, probing the depth with a long pole to determine where the deepest parts were. He marked his route with branches torn from trees, and once he had an almost navigable channel, he would divert the current with more branches and rocks to form a route deep enough for his boat.

The best known of Deacon's tramp steamers were *Josie*, a sidewheeler built in 1890; *Pathfinder*, another sidewheeler built in 1903; and *Marion*, a single-screw tug dating from about 1910. They were all little tugs with shallow draft—no more than two feet—but they were powerful enough to do the job at hand. *Marion* often had a loaded barge or scow tied to one side and still managed to keep moving. Deacon's first two tugs both had "an upright boiler; they ran on gears, no drive shaft, just one small gear, to a larger one, to the paddlewheel[s]." *Marion* was somewhat different. Her single propeller was only three feet in diameter and had to drive enormous loads through the water with whatever power the less-than-perfect engines could supply. One of Deacon's grandsons reported, "Her engines weren't marine engines; they were makeshift . . . and exhausted to atmosphere, not into a condenser. She was quite wasteful on fuel and you could hear her puffin' away to beat the band."

Despite having a reputation for being cranky and lacking good business skills (he had grand ideas but was not clever with money), Richard Deacon was temperate and a good citizen who served on Prince Albert's town council. He was known for taking groups of Prince Albert children and local church groups on excursions. He was also opinionated, competitive to a fault and not averse to condemning his rivals for their lack of professionalism or their river-running skills, especially if they happened to beat him to a job.

One of the bigger tramps was the 100-foot-long sternwheeler *City of Prince Albert*, built in 1907. She had a single deck, a 24-foot beam and a utilitarian but far from attractive superstructure topped by a thick smokestack. Much of her time was spent hauling lumber to mills on the North Saskatchewan. Theodore Barris wrote, "Every day the *City* manoeuvred four rafts, each with 1,400 logs, upriver from the Little Red River."

The side-wheel steamer *Cheyenne,* owned by the HBC, was typical of prairie river steamers in the late 1800s and early 1900s. She is seen here on the Assiniboine River discharging cargo for Upper Fort Garry in 1874. HBC ARCHIVES/ARCHIVES OF MANITOBA 1987/363-C-24/1

City of Prince Albert carried an unusual feature. Standing tall ahead of her smokestack was a single timber cut from a fir tree, known as a "grouser." Measuring 26 feet long and 14 by 16 inches thick, with a steel-capped point, the grouser was an innovative way to anchor a big steamboat in the North Saskatchewan River's currents. The grouser could be dropped through a well in the steamboat's hull and stabbed into the riverbed to keep the boat stationary. When it was time to move on, a hoist lifted the grouser up through the well so it could be secured in a vertical position ready for the next stop.

Captain Fred Coates and his entrepreneur partner Rufus Mosher built a sternwheeler in Prince Albert in 1904. Ignoring the fact that there had already been a steamer with the same name, they called their vessel *Alberta* and put her to work as a freighter on the North Saskatchewan River. On summer weekends, the drudgery of carrying cargo from port to port—and loading and unloading it every day—was alleviated with excursion parties, which included dancing to an orchestra. Those evening cruises, carrying anywhere from 50 to 100 revellers, added fifty cents per person to the company's coffers. The sale of snacks and ice cream supplemented the income.

Perhaps *Alberta's* most bizarre and ungainly cargo was a 100-foot-long gold dredge. Shipped overland in pieces from New York in 1905, the dredge was assembled in Prince Albert, and Coates and Mosher were entrusted with its delivery to Gunn's Island, 17 miles away. Connected to *Alberta* by heavy-duty tow lines, the dredge was dragged upriver on an overnight voyage, grounding on sand bars as it went. It was a tough job, but no more than the crews expected.

The working life of a tramp steamer's skipper and crew was always hard. They worked long hours and often for little pay. To balance this, however, was the romance of often not knowing where the boat would be going from one day to the next or what cargo she might be carrying. To the adventurous men who served on river tramps, the hard life was a good life. All that gradually came to an end in 1913. The railways carried more and more people and freight. The economy went into a slump, and the threat of war surfaced in Europe. There was no demand for river tramps any more.

9

Yukon Gold

WHEN GEORGE CARMACK, SKOOKUM JIM and Tagish Charlie found a small fortune in gold at Rabbit Creek near Dawson City in Yukon Territory on August 17, 1896, their shouts of jubilation were heard by very few other men. Prospectors had been taking out placer gold from Yukon's rivers and creeks for over a decade, but nothing had equalled this find. The news spread slowly across the territory, although it gathered momentum with each spoken phrase: "A large amount of gold has been found in a creek running into the Klondike River. It is the big strike. It is a bonanza."

The rest of the world knew nothing of the find, but the news would not be long in getting out. When word of the gold strike reached Vancouver, Seattle and San Francisco, it sent out shock waves that reverberated around the world. Gold! The very word heated passionate blood to the boiling point and created a high fever: gold fever. Soon thousands of would-be gold miners and prospectors were setting out for Yukon from homes near and far. The Klondike gold rush had begun.

For most of the excited adventurers, getting to the Klondike Valley was a supreme test of stamina, endurance and willpower. Many would fall by the wayside. Many would die. For those with the courage to go on—and they were a multitude—the choice of routes was dictated by their financial well-being at the start.

The busiest route was by sea up the Inside Passage to Skagway, Alaska. From there, the prospectors had a choice of the tortuous 45-mile-long White Pass or the forbidding Chilkoot Pass. The White Pass looked easier due to its lower altitude—it wasn't. More than 5,000 men and a few women attempted the route in 1897, and a high proportion failed. The Chilkoot Pass also took a huge toll. Despite the impossibly steep angle of the upper sections of the trail, where only men and mountain goats could maintain a footing, more than 20,000 men hauled their equipment over the top and beyond to reach the goldfields. Those with limited cash had to rely on their ingenuity and build their own carts and boats and take a different route.

Edmonton, Alberta, experienced its own boom because

of the gold rush. Although it was still 1,600 miles short of the Klondike, it was only 180 miles from the new trans-Canada rail line and was seen as a useful jumping-off point for what would become known as "The All-Canadian Route" to the riches of the gold-bearing rivers.

The All-Canadian Route was not for the faint of heart. After purchasing their outfits in Edmonton, eager men and more than a few women trekked north to Athabasca Landing, 90 miles away. From there, they either booked passage on steamboats along rivers and over lakes to reach the distant peaks of the northern extremes of the Rocky Mountains, or they built their own transport.

The water section of the route took them north down the Athabasca River to Fort Chipewyan at the western end of Lake Athabasca. From there, they followed the Slave River, always heading north and with a lengthy run of deadly rapids to avoid halfway along. At Fort Resolution on the south shore of Great Slave Lake, the prospectors turned west to the beginning of the great Mackenzie River. After about 1,000 miles on the Mackenzie, they reached the vast delta on the edge of the Arctic Ocean. There they turned inland again to find a way up the Peel River and through the passes guarded by the last heights of the Canadian Rockies. As the Peel became more turbulent, they were forced to take to the land and find an accessible pass to lead them down to the Stewart River and a final downhill water ride to Dawson City.

Some of the gold seekers displayed remarkable ingenuity. Two men converted what appeared to be a long, narrow rowing skiff to steam power. They added a flimsy paddlewheel placed well aft of the rudder and a steam boiler in front of the steering position and set course from Athabasca Landing for Yukon Territory in the spring of 1898. Whether or not they reached the Klondike is unknown. Another pair, Jim Wallwork and Charles Roberts, purchased a small flat-bottomed steamboat on the North Saskatchewan River, hauled it overland to Athabasca Landing and set off for the Klondike, also in the spring of 1898. Their partnership did not survive the journey, but Wallwork persevered and reached Dawson alone in July 1899, 16 months after he set out from Edmonton. Four other men built or otherwise took possession of a boxy old scow named *Boston*. They added a roof structure, installed a boiler and the required mechanical parts, added a stern paddlewheel and away they went. There were many others who attempted to make similar river journeys. An unknown number succeeded, but most who tried the route failed.

It was less of an ordeal for the wealthy. The financially favoured few followed the rich man's route: by sea from a west-coast port to St. Michael at the mouth of the Yukon River and then upstream on paddle-steamers to Dawson City. By the summer of 1897, there were too many people in the Dawson area and little food available. There were said to be five steamboats en route up the Yukon loaded with food,

Getting to the Klondike often required inventive and unusual transportation. These men built a small sternwheel paddle-steamer from a rowing skiff and set off from Athabasca Landing in 1898. There is no record of whether they reached Yukon or not.

but no one knew where they were. In fact, the five boats had become stranded in shallow water on the Yukon flats, 350 miles short of Dawson. The town residents, business-men and miners faced starvation as another harsh winter approached.

It is believed that close to 300 steamboats of varying descriptions operated on the Yukon River, in Yukon and in Alaska, between the late 1800s and the mid-1950s. Of those, *Portus B. Weare* is said to have been the first steamboat to reach Dawson City after the news of the gold strike broke in the south. *Portus B. Weare*, 175 feet long and 400 gross tons, was in the right place at the right time. She had been working on the Yukon since 1892.

When *Portus B. Weare* steamed into sight one evening in late September 1897 she was greeted by enthusiastic crowds, all hoping the boat and those that came after her would be loaded with food supplies to help them through the coming winter. They were disappointed. *Weare* was followed two days later by the slightly smaller *Bella*. Neither boat carried food; both were laden with whisky and hardware, the latter presumably for mining purposes. When the two boats left a few days later for the run downstream to Fort Yukon, they carried disappointed prospectors trying to get out of the North before starvation and the harsh realities of snow and ice finished them off.

After a dreadful winter, and as the first week of June 1898 came to an end, a motley fleet of small boats began pouring into Dawson from the south. Among them were makeshift rafts, canoes, rowboats and sailboats—anything that would float. The 134-ton steamboat *May West* arrived at Dawson City on June 8. Five thousand people lined the banks of the Yukon River to greet and celebrate her arrival. *May West* was followed by the much smaller *Bellingham* five days later. *Bellingham*, only 35 feet long, had been built on Bennett Lake in Yukon Territory in 1897 and was the first steamboat to navigate the upper Yukon River.

The Canadian Pacific Railway company (CPR) was quick to see the opportunities for growth into a new enterprise. In 1898, they advertised their preferred route to the Klondike, which stressed the value of the CPR's railway network: "Take the Canadian Pacific Railway to Vancouver or Victoria, B.C.; thence ocean steamer via the inland channel to Fort Wrangel; river steamer up the Stikine River to Glenora or Telegraph Creek; pack trail or wagon road to Teslin Lake, and river steamer down the Hootalinqua and Lewes rivers to Fort Selkirk and Dawson City." The CPR quoted the total distance as 1,542 miles.

At that time, the CPR did not have ships operating on the Inside Passage, nor did they have any vessels on the Stikine River. The company's directors soon took care of that gap in their service by purchasing two small ocean-going steamers from England's Union Line: the 4,399-ton *Tartar* and a smaller sister ship, *Athenian*, at 3,877 tons. Both ships went into service on the Inside Passage in the spring of 1898. Steamboats for service on the Stikine River were not so readily available. They had to be built, and to keep expenses within reasonable limits, they had to be built locally, in Vancouver or a Washington shipyard.

The CPR planned to have 12 sternwheelers in use on the Stikine within a couple of years. They were *Constantine*, *Dalton*, *Duchesnay*, *G.M. Dawson*, *Hamlin*, *McConnell*, *Minto*, *Moyie*, *Ogilvie*, *Schwatka*, *Tyrrell* and *Walsh*. All were equipped with one funnel, except *Constantine*, which was designed primarily as a freighter and sported twin smokestacks. Four of the boats were ordered from a

Port Blakely, Washington, shipyard. The rest were to be constructed in Canada, four of them in the False Creek shipyards. It was an ambitious plan that did not prove to be worthwhile.

Despite the speed with which the CPR had their stern-wheelers built, another company beat them to the punch. When the ice cleared off the Stikine in May 1898, the CPR was not quite ready. The rival steamboat *Ramona* was the first to get away from Fort Wrangel and nose her way upriver. Two other non-CPR boats followed. The first CPR sternwheeler on the Stikine was *Hamlin*. She was followed by *Ogilvie*, which soon became recognized as the fastest steamboat on that river.

The Stikine River flows from the snowfields and glaciers of the Cassiar Mountains, north and east of the town of Telegraph Creek. Like most rivers spawned in high mountains, it demands the utmost respect from those who would run its course. After travelling on *Ogilvie*'s first round trip on the Stikine, a rather awed passenger wrote:

Twelve miles from the boundary [the US-Canada border] is Great Glacier . . . extending 7½ miles along the river bank and back as far as the eye can reach . . . The Big Canyon, about 80 miles from the mouth of the river, is the finest part of the whole trip. Here, for a mile and a quarter, the water rushes through a narrow gorge, a mountain torrent, and on both sides the rocky cliffs rise straight from the water's edge 60 to 70 feet. The real power of this is not realized until

the down [stream] trip is made, when the steamer rushes
through with the current at a rate of 20 miles per hour.

Gold fever, exciting though it might have been, was a
capricious malady. By the time many of the steamboats were
ready for service, the Klondike gold rush was just about over.
The hordes of prospectors travelling to and from Dawson
City had slowed to a trickle. The Klondike was no longer
big news; instead a new rush had begun. Gold had been
found far to the west on the beaches of Nome, where the
Bering Sea washed the sands clean. The CPR found its new
sternwheelers redundant before their careers had begun.

As the passenger and freight traffic on the Stikine dwin-
dled, the CPR's directors made a drastic decision. Only
three months after the Stikine service started, they ceased
operations on that river. On the Inside Passage, the two ex–
Union Line steamers, *Tartar* and *Athenian*, also proved to
be unprofitable. They were both withdrawn from the route
and subsequently sold after making only six round-trip voyages each to Fort Wrangel. The sternwheelers *McConnell*
and *Ogilvie* were broken up. *Hamlin* and *Duchesnay* were
sold. *Constantine, Dalton, Walsh, Schwatka* and *Tyrrell* had
never left their shipyards. Only *Tyrrell* survived to work in
the North. She made the long ocean voyage from Vancouver
to St. Michael on the Bering Sea and then up the Yukon
River, where she remained in service until the 1920s. The
other vessels were sold or transferred to other CPR regions.

Moyie and *Minto* became fixtures on British Columbia's Kootenay Lake for many years. *Moyie*, in fact, is still very much in evidence as a historic museum of a bygone era. She stands in solitary splendour on the western shore of Kootenay Lake at Kaslo and is cared for by the Kootenay Lake Historical Society.

Even though the CPR had not made a success of northern shipping, others certainly had. The Alaska Commercial Company placed three huge paddle-steamers on the Yukon River in the summer of 1898. *Hannah*, *Sarah* and *Susie* were all 223 feet long and weighed in at 1,130 gross tons. That summer, dozens of steamers could be seen on the river at Dawson or close by. Though many were ornate floating palaces, few could equal the Alaska Commercial Company's three ladies. They had a style all their own and served their owners well until they were sold to the White Pass & Yukon Route railway company in 1914.

The White Pass & Yukon Route launched its first steamboat on the Yukon River in 1901. The company quickly expanded its nautical capacity until it owned more than 80 steamboats between 1914 and 1921. Those boats carried passengers and freight along 2,000 miles of Alaska and Yukon rivers and lakes. Some of the boats were built on the lower mainland of British Columbia, on Vancouver Island, in Washington and in Oregon. Many travelled to the upper reaches of the Yukon under their own steam out of west-coast ports from Portland to Vancouver. Others were transported up the sheltered Inside Passage and man-handled in pieces over the daunting White Pass Trail and assembled in Whitehorse. Once afloat on the Yukon River, most of them served the Whitehorse to Dawson City route.

The Klondike gold strike boosted the steamboat era on the Yukon River and paved the way for a few decades of steamer traffic in Alaska and Yukon. Without the gold rush and its aftermath, it is unlikely that there would have been the commercial requirement for so many steamboats to be committed to the region. The last steamboat to operate on the Yukon River was the sternwheeler *Keno*. She is now a museum on land at Dawson, beside the river she worked on for 38 years.

10

North toward the Arctic

THE ATHABASCA RIVER BEGINS ITS long journey in the meltwater streams of the Athabasca Glacier as it glides at a snail's pace down a long, wide valley from the Columbia Icefields. Tumbling down a narrow channel across the toe of the glacier, the icy, embryonic river widens and flows roughly north along the east side of the Continental Divide through Jasper National Park, then gradually curves northeast. Northwest of Edmonton it changes direction, as it will do many times, but always reaching for the north and hurrying to shed its waters born of ice and snow into the Arctic Ocean. For the early part of its journey, the Athabasca builds power and speed as it runs over rapids and falls. It becomes navigable to shallow-draft working boats near Athabasca Landing.

The small riverside settlement of Athabasca Landing, a handful of log buildings—and little else—due north of Edmonton, can lay claim to seeing the first steamboat to ply the Athabasca River. The hull, decking and upperworks of *Midnight Sun* were built at Athabasca Landing, but her rotund boiler was fabricated in Edmonton. It had to be rolled overland for 90 miles, pulled by six horses. Few obstacles could thwart the intentions of steamboat men for long.

A subsequent steamer, *Northern Sun*, carried journalists and entrepreneurs on a four-week, 2,000-mile journey along the Athabasca and Peace river systems to show what the northland had to offer for those prepared to make the move. Athabasca Landing (now just called Athabasca) became the focal point for transportation to the North. Most of the freight and passengers went slowly to their destinations by steamboat, through clouds of mosquitoes, past swimming bears and over rapids.

The waters of the Peace River also begin their long pathway to the Arctic Ocean in the snowfields of the Canadian Rockies. The Peace is born as the Finlay River. At Finlay Forks it is joined by half a dozen other small rivers to become the exuberant misnamed giant threading its way across northern British Columbia and Alberta. It meets the Athabasca River at the western end of Lake Athabasca, and the two join their considerable forces to become the Slave River, which runs almost due north to reach Great Slave Lake.

The Peace River is navigable from its confluence with the Athabasca as far west as Hudson's Hope. Many steamboats, large and small, worked on the Peace. Following two years of employment on the Athabasca River for the HBC, the 136-foot-long sternwheeler *Athabasca River* was winched up the Vermilion Chutes in 1914 and served all the way to Hudson's Hope until 1919. Her career as a steamship ended when she was converted to a barge. One of the Peace River's most famous steamboats was the redoubtable wooden sternwheeler *D.A. Thomas*, built in 1916 at Peace River, Alberta. She was a fraction under 162 feet long and 40 feet across her beam. Powered by two Polson steam engines, she was sold to the HBC in 1924 and continued in service on the Peace until she was holed and sunk in 1927. Raised soon after, *D.A. Thomas* had only a few years of life ahead. She was wrecked while running the Vermilion Chutes in 1930.

Steamboats on the Peace River began to be phased out in the early 1930s. The remaining vessels, owned by the HBC, were transferred to the Slave and Mackenzie Rivers for service to the Arctic.

The mighty Mackenzie River, which carries the waters of the Athabasca and Peace Rivers on the final leg of their journey, is 1,000 miles long between Great Slave Lake and its Arctic delta, and up to three miles wide in places. It travels through land that is the traditional home of the Dene First Nation, who call the Mackenzie River *Deh Cho*.

The broad expanse of Vermilion Chutes was a formidable barrier to steamboat navigation on the Athabasca River, but the chutes could be run—by experts. PEACE RIVER MUSEUM 87.1492.048

A Scotsman, Alexander Mackenzie, was the first non-Native to travel the full length of the river that now bears his name. Mackenzie was employed as a chief factor for the North West Company (later to become part of the HBC) at Fort Chipewyan. In 1789, he ventured north and west with four canoes and a team of Native paddlers to explore a mighty river he had heard about from locals. Mackenzie hoped it would lead him to the Pacific Ocean, but instead he found himself in the Arctic.

The Liard River joins the Mackenzie a little over 150 miles west of Great Slave Lake. Both waterways saw considerable activity during the steamboat era. At the close of the 19th century, the HBC had steamboats, such as the screw-driven *Wrigley*, working on the Mackenzie and supplying settlements for 1,000 miles or more. *Wrigley* was the first steamboat in regular service on the Mackenzie River. She was built at Fort Smith for the HBC in 1886 and worked on the river each open-water season until she was retired in 1911 and replaced by the large sternwheeler *Mackenzie River*.

Steamboats continued to work on the Mackenzie River well into the first half of the 20th century. The HBC sternwheeler *Distributor*, for example, ran a regular route from Great Slave Lake to Aklavik on the southwest side of the Mackenzie delta for many years. *Distributor* was designed for service on the Slave and Mackenzie Rivers and was built in 1920 for Lampson and Hubbard. She was a large vessel, as befitted the size of the river she would mainly travel. From bow to sternwheel, she was 200 feet long, and she displaced 875 tons. Despite her great size, *Distributor* drew only four feet of water. In 1924, she was sold to the HBC and employed on the 1,300-mile run from Fort Smith, on the Slave River, to Aklavik, on the Mackenzie delta. This long journey could take anywhere from four to five weeks in each direction, depending on weather conditions. Due to the shortness of the navigating season on the Mackenzie, *Distributor* only managed two round trips to the Arctic outposts each summer.

Like many other big, shallow-draft sternwheelers, *Distributor* was top-heavy, not a desirable design element

The sternwheel steamer *Distributor* served the widely separated settlements on the Slave River, Great Slave Lake and the long Mackenzie River for the HBC, among others, from 1920 until the early 1950s. FRED JACKSON FONDS, NWT ARCHIVES N-1979-004: 0195

for any kind of boat. Above the waterline stood a large superstructure that contained two steam engines, passengers' cabins and two saloons. Above those were the wheelhouse and a chart room. Great Slave Lake and the Mackenzie River can be whipped up into substantial waves by high winds, and under those conditions, *Distributor* could be uncontrollable. In addition to her own bulk, the sternwheeler often pushed as many as four or five heavily laden barges ahead of her, attached to the bow and each other by a series of strong steel cables. The crew of 32 had to be ready to rearrange the weight by moving cargo around the main vessel or changing the configuration of the barges to maintain stability in rough weather.

Under the HBC banner, *Distributor* steamed from the foot of the Slave River Rapids at Fort Smith, down the Slave to Fort Resolution to Great Slave Lake. If the weather was good and the lake calm, *Distributor* would then cruise west along the south shore of the lake to call at Hay River before entering the Mackenzie River. The Mackenzie is very shallow for the first few miles after leaving the lake—no more than a few feet deep in places—hence the need for the steamboats to have such a shallow draft.

En route downriver, depending on freight and passenger requirements, the steamer called at Fort Providence, Fort Simpson, Wrigley, Fort Norman, Norman Wells, Fort Good Hope, Arctic Red River and Aklavik—up the Peel Channel on the west side of the delta.

In 1937, *Distributor* had the distinct honour of carrying Lord Tweedsmuir, the Governor General of Canada, and his party from Fort Smith to Aklavik. In private life, Lord Tweedsmuir was the well-known author John Buchan, who penned the popular thriller *The Thirty-Nine Steps*, among scores of other novels. On that occasion, *Distributor* was at her best and made the long voyage from Fort Smith to Aklavik in a mere 11 days, a record for the time, and put the party of dignitaries five days ahead of schedule. It was a fast run, but the crew and passengers still found time to have some fun en route. On crossing the Arctic Circle after a stop

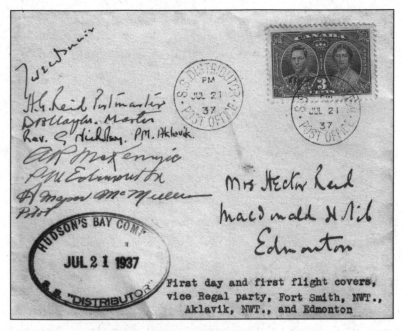

Lord Tweedsmuir, the Governor General of Canada, travelled the Mackenzie River on SS *Distributor* in July 1937. This signed envelope is a "first flight and first day cover" to commemorate the occasion.
COURTESY OF ANDREW LIPTAK

at Fort Norman, the Governor General was introduced to a special northern eminence: Santa Claus. The ceremony took place on board as the steamboat travelled north. William Galbraith, Tweedsmuir's biographer, reported:

His enfrosted majesty, King Santa Claus (played by a young Hudson's Bay Company employee, Richard Bonnycastle) the first emperor of the snows, grand seigneur of the Aurora

Borealis and warden of the midnight sun, in the name of
the polar bear, the caribou, the teepee and the kayak, (gave
leave to the Governor General) to cross the Arctic circle
and be admitted into the most enviable order of seekers for
the north.

Lord Tweedsmuir seemed to enjoy his voyage down
the Mackenzie on *Distributor*, although his impressions
of Aklavik were less than pleasant. He thought Aklavik as
a settlement was a "complete mistake." He was not much
more impressed by the Mackenzie delta, referring to it as
"the most sinister place I have ever seen" and likening it to
"the no-man's land between the trenches in the war."

The Governor General and his party left Aklavik on an
RCAF aircraft. *Distributor* and her crew returned to their
regular work, retracing their course back up the Mackenzie,
fighting the strong current all the way to Great Slave Lake.
Distributor continued in service on the Mackenzie River
until the mid-1950s.

CHAPTER

11

British Columbia's Big River Canyons

A DULL ROAR SPREADS ACROSS the land like a distant storm. Unlike thunder, which announces itself with intermittent bangs and crashes, this drum roll of massive proportions never fades—not even in the depths of winter when snow and ice shroud the surrounding forests and cling to the cold granite of steep canyon walls. The roar is constant and has been so since long before man walked on this part of the earth.

Most of mainland British Columbia's big rivers, which create the eternal roar, begin their often turbulent journeys in the rugged heights of the Rocky Mountains. Fed by glacial meltwater, most of them are in a hurry to reach the distant oceans. To get there, they must carve serpentine routes across a wild landscape of lush woodlands alternating with steep and dangerous canyons of harsh granite. These are not waterways one would normally associate with commercial river transport, yet in the late 1800s and early 1900s, sternwheel paddle-steamers operated successfully on many of British Columbia's largest and wildest rivers, such as the Fraser, Thompson, Columbia, Stikine and Skeena. These rivers, then as now, were fast-moving with long stretches of whitewater cascading down rapids and through narrow canyons. It required skill, panache and daring to navigate shallow-draft steamboats, in either direction, on rivers racing down and through mountains to the valleys below.

The Fraser River flows out of the Rocky Mountains above Yellowhead Pass near the massive snow-capped bulk of Mount Robson and travels 850 miles to reach the distant west coast at Vancouver. On its long journey to the Pacific Ocean, it collects the Nechako, Quesnel, Chilcotin and Thompson Rivers. The Upper Fraser, between Soda Creek and Tête Jaune Cache, is a 472-mile-long stretch of river that alternates between being wide and fast-flowing and tumbling in a mess of whitewater through long, deep gaps carved in granite. Bordered by thick forests, the river was the obvious choice for moving freight from one place to another—if it could be done safely. Three major areas with difficult rapids gave cause for concern: Fort George Canyon, 15 miles south of Fort George (now Prince George); Giscome Rapids, near Huble Homestead; and the Grand Canyon of the Upper

Fraser. The latter, a ragged scar running southeast to northwest, was carved by the Fraser River.

Over a mile long, the Grand Canyon is distinguished by a series of extraordinary features. Green's Rock, a large prominence, sits in the narrowest part of the canyon just round a tight bend from the upper rapids. A couple of falls come next, which used to be more of a hazard until they were dynamited to oblivion in 1912. Between the upper and lower rapids is a lake, a breathing space before the lower rapids and a large whirlpool that can extend the width of the canyon when the water level is high. The lower canyon is littered with sandbars in the area of Alexander's Island. They are particularly obvious at low water.

River scows and big canoes were in use on the Upper Fraser long before steamboats ventured that far. Those small boats weren't safe, and the loss of life among rivermen in the rapids was appalling, but it didn't stop the men from running the whitewater.

One of the first steamboats on the Upper Fraser was the attractive little sternwheeler *Enterprise*. Built at Four Mile Creek in 1863 for service between Soda Creek and Quesnel, a distance of no more than 40 miles, *Enterprise* was a fixture on that part of the Upper Fraser system until 1871. She was the first of 12 steamers to work on the Upper Fraser. In 1871, her owners sent *Enterprise* to attempt to navigate the Nechako River west from Fort George, up the Stuart River to Stuart Lake, then through Trembleur and Takla Lakes to

Enterprise was an elegant little sternwheel steamer working on the Upper Fraser River. She is seen here at Soda Creek.
ROYAL BC MUSEUM, BC ARCHIVES A-03908

reach the Omineca goldfields. *Enterprise* didn't make it all the way to her destination, but she did make it as far as Trembleur Lake, where she was damaged and had to be abandoned.

Although at least two steamers worked the Soda Creek to Quesnel route between 1863 and 1886 (*Enterprise* and *Victoria*), none operated up to Fort George, or beyond to the Grand Canyon area, or even farther to Tête Jaune Cache. The most obvious reason was the rapids at Fort George Canyon, 15 miles south of the town. As a consequence, Fort George had no steamboat service until 1908, when the 12-year-old, 110-foot-long *Charlotte* blew in from Quesnel and introduced passenger and freight traffic to the area.

Charlotte's skipper, Captain Alexander, found Fort George Canyon a serious challenge to his skills as a steamboat man. Two years after his first run through the defile, he almost lost his steamer. The crew were winching *Charlotte* upstream when the towing cable slipped off a steel pin driven into the wall of the canyon for the purpose. Before Alexander could react, the current had taken charge and bounced the boat off a rock, puncturing her hull. Even so, the captain regained control and managed to get her safely down to the southern end of the canyon, although she had a few feet of water in the hold. No passengers were involved in the incident, as it was customary for them to walk the portage route past the whitewater.

One month later, *Charlotte* was in trouble again at the head of the same canyon. This time she was heading south to Quesnel while the passengers were still on board, and they were scared. The *Fort George Herald* reported the accident:

The wind and current were too strong at a dangerous point and it was impossible to control the course of the steamer. She was forced at full speed bow first onto a rock, causing a collision of such force as to stave in the stem post. The jar caused a shifting forward of the boiler several inches, breaking the steam connections and enveloping the vessel and passengers in a cloud of steam.

Again, the skill of the captain combined with the expertise of the chief engineer and help from the crew saved the steamer. They managed to moor *Charlotte* and set about making repairs. Within a few hours, the boiler had been moved back into its proper seat and secured, the steam pipes had been repaired and the passengers, now calm, were able to enjoy the rest of their river voyage.

But *Charlotte* hadn't finished with her difficulties. Another few weeks passed, and she was once again running down the Fort George Canyon, this time under a different captain. As is normal in whitewater in a confined space, the boat was tossed around and must have scraped over a rock without the abrasion being heard or felt by the crew. The first indication that there was a problem came when someone noticed the hull was filling with water. By the time she reached the southern end of the canyon, *Charlotte* was sinking and in danger of rolling over to starboard. The captain and crew saved the passengers and the steamer by running *Charlotte* ashore.

The ill-fated competitor *Chilco* arrived on the upper Fraser in the summer of 1909 as *Nechacco*. She was the first steamer to navigate through the Grand Canyon. She then continued as far as Goat Rapids to unload her cargo. *Nechacco* made valiant journeys on the Upper Fraser as well as up and down the rapids of the Nechako River. Due to damage sustained in too many collisions with rocks, she was rebuilt and received a new name: *Chilco*. She didn't last long under her new persona. *Chilco* was wrecked in Cottonwood Canyon while en route to Quesnel for repairs in late April 1911. Her boiler blew up and, with no steam, she was uncontrollable. She drifted into ice in the canyon and broke apart.

The upper Fraser was a busy river, and F.J. Barnard, a notable British Columbian businessman in the first decade of the 20th century, saw its potential. He owned a fleet of stagecoaches operating along the banks of the Fraser River between Ashcroft and Fort George. To haul those stages, Barnard also owned some 200 horses. Aware of the obvious freight- and passenger-carrying potential of riverboats, Barnard commissioned two sternwheelers, *B.X.* and *BC Express*, to add to his transportation potential. *B.X.* was 127.5 feet long and was built at Soda Creek and launched in mid-May 1910. Barnard's advertisement for his company's services read, "BX Connects Quesnel with the Railways." Under the heading "BX Steamers," he advertised:

> From Soda Creek and Quesnel to Fort George and all points ahead of steel to the G.T.P. at Tête Jaune Cache. These steamers are the fastest and most comfortable on the upper Fraser. Spacious smoking and dining saloons, ladies' drawing rooms, bathrooms, spotlessly clean staterooms. Electrically lighted and steam heated. Excellent cuisine, with moderate charges. Splendid freight accommodation. Full particulars from local agent.

The sternwheeler *B.X.* slides between the rocks of Fort George Canyon on the Upper Fraser River between Fort George and Quesnel in 1911. ROYAL BC MUSEUM, BC ARCHIVES I-57868

The advertisement may not have been well written, but it achieved Barnard's purpose. In 1910, her first year of operations, *B.X.* carried 138,000 pounds of freight on a single voyage to Fort George. In May of the following year, *B.X.* steamed into Fort George at night with "over a hundred passengers" and 85,000 pounds of freight. A newspaper report stated that all passenger accommodation on the *B.X.* "was booked for several trips ahead."

BC Express joined *B.X.* on the Fraser in June 1912. Just over 140 feet long, she was built for traffic between Fort George and Tête Jaune Cache. That journey of over 300 miles required considerable skills from steamboat captains.

BC Express's skipper was equal to the test. The *Fort George Herald* reported on the sternwheeler's first run to Tête Jaune Cache with a complimentary tone: "The new steamboat negotiated the lower Grand Canyon without any difficulty. She streamed through the whirlpool and up into the lake that divides the canyon in two without the aid of any lines."

The Grand Canyon wasn't the only hazard en route. Giscome Rapids stretches seven miles and, like the Grand Canyon, has claimed many lives. Many unskilled canoeists, scow operators and rafters came to grief in its whitewater.

The Skeena River in northern British Columbia was the setting for many steamboat tales. The second-largest river in the province, the Skeena, flows at high speed for 354 miles from the snowfields of the Spatsizi Plateau, high in the Coast Mountains, to the Pacific Ocean at Prince Rupert. It is a wild river and unnavigable in its upper reaches. Even lower down it is not a river for amateurs.

The HBC sternwheeler *Mount Royal* was lost, along with six crewmen, when she was rolled over by currents in Kitselas Canyon in July 1907. A few years earlier, *Mount Royal* had competed aggressively against the slightly older sternwheeler *Hazelton*. The captains of the two well-matched boats raced each other to and from Prince Rupert to Hazelton. The sight of the two steamers thundering up or down the river side by side would have been a stirring experience. In 1904, the rivalry became so fierce that *Hazelton*'s skipper, Captain Bonser, rammed *Mount Royal* more than once as she steamed past. Captain Johnson at *Mount Royal*'s helm lost control, and his boat fell behind; all on board could see *Hazelton*'s sternwheel pounding at the river as she drew away. To end the dangerous rivalry, the HBC purchased *Hazelton* and retired her. She ended her days at Prince Rupert as the local yacht club's social centre.

There is no doubt that the most bizarre accident ever to happen to a river steamboat occurred in British Columbia. The wooden sternwheeler *Gwendoline*, 63 feet, 6 inches long, was built in 1893 for service on the upper Columbia River. In June 1899, she was loaded onto a flatbed railcar and hauled down past Kootenai Falls. Somehow she tipped off the flatbed while it was crossing a trestle and tumbled 70 feet into a canyon. *Gwendoline* landed on her back, her keel in the air, and was completely wrecked.

In addition to steamboats on the major rivers, British Columbia's long, narrow lakes in the Okanagan and Kootenay regions had their own working fleets of steamboats that operated regular services between lakefront towns for over six decades. There are enough stories associated with these lake-bound steamboats for a book of their own.

CHAPTER

12

Steamboats in Ontario

A QUICK LOOK AT A MAP of eastern Canada shows that Ontario is a province particularly well endowed with rivers and lakes. They were used for hundreds of years as trade and hunting routes by Native peoples and later by Hudson's Bay Company fur traders. Later, in the 19th and early 20th centuries, wherever there was a navigable river or a lake deep enough for shipping, and a few towns scattered along their shores needing service, there were steamboats.

The Ottawa is the second-largest river in eastern Canada, eclipsed only by the St. Lawrence. It flows out of the wilderness highlands of Quebec on a westerly course before it turns south to form part of the boundary between

Quebec and Ontario. At Mattawa, south of Temiscaming, it becomes a big river and speeds east. Separating Ottawa and Hull, it continues east until it spends itself in the St. Lawrence River on the south side of Montreal. Its overall length is 795 miles.

The first steamer on the Ottawa River was the side-wheel paddle-steamer *Lady Colborne*. Built of wood in Aylmer in 1832, *Lady Colborne* was a 100-foot-long passenger steamer with a beam of 34 feet, including the paddlewheels. She worked on the Ottawa between Aylmer and Fitzroy four times a week in each direction for the seven months that the river was open each year. *Lady Colborne* was joined on the river by the 77-foot-long *George Buchanan* in 1836. The latter ship, built in Arnprior, Ontario, worked above Chat's Falls, while *Lady Colborne* stayed to the east. On the days the two steamers were not required for scheduled passenger services, they were used for towing and occasionally for private parties. Ten years later, the 140-foot-long *Emerald* slid down the ways at Aylmer. Built for the Union Forwarding and Railway Company, the two-deck steamer was a definite step up for the company. She had staterooms for comfortable overnight accommodation, plus a spacious dining room and a bar. Three months later, the company launched a sister ship, *Oregon*, above Chat's Falls.

At one time it was possible to travel the Ottawa River on steamers from Montreal as far as Mattawa, although this required many changes of boats and other transportation en route. In his book *Ottawa Waterway*, Robert Legget wrote of the complexity of the journey from Aylmer toward Mattawa:

> Breakfast was enjoyed during the leisurely sail on Lac Deschênes with several stops at small settlements on the way. The ride around Chat's Falls on the horse-railroad took about twenty minutes, at the end of which one would board the *Alliance*, due to sail at 11:00 a.m. Midday dinner was taken in the "palatial" dining saloon of this Chat's Lake vessel. If it was possible to get up [river] as far as Gould's Wharf (Portage du Fort), one then took the waiting stagecoach for the twelve mile ride through the forests to Cobden, there to board the *Muskrat* for the final sail to near Pembroke. Another meal, described as "tea", was taken on this small vessel, completing the experience of enjoying three meals in one day on three different steamboats. Pembroke would be reached in the early evening. To go any further upriver after spending the night at Pembroke, one had to start at 1:00 p.m. next day on the *Pembroke* or the *Pontiac* for the sail to Des Joachims, where an overnight stay could be made in another of the riverside hotels.

In 1856 *Lady Colborne* was sold to a Montreal company and put to work on the St. Lawrence River between Montreal and Quebec City under the name *Crescent*.

By the 1860s, the Union Forwarding and Railway Company had increased their fleet of steamers to nine boats. Competition had arrived too, in the shape of the Upper Ottawa Steamboat Company, as well as railway lines extending farther and farther along the south and west banks of the river. As a result of the competition created by the increased transportation offerings along the Ottawa River, the Union Forwarding fleet ceased carrying passengers on their ships at the close of the 1879 season.

On the east side of Ottawa, another shipping business, the Ottawa River Navigational Company, had been confident enough in the future to launch a new iron steamer, *Peerless*, near Queen's Wharf on May 16, 1872. Thousands of onlookers watched as the 200-foot-long *Peerless* slid down the ways to begin passenger and freight service on the Ottawa to Grenville route. A newspaper report from the day commented on the "rapidly increasing traffic on the [Ottawa] river."

While the Ottawa River was perhaps better known as a commercial waterway, the Niagara River has also achieved considerable fame. The Niagara thunders over the two mighty cataracts of Niagara Falls, a significant tourist site for over 180 years, which gives it a certain romance and cachet.

In September 1827, a bizarre and pointlessly cruel stunt was performed at the Horseshoe Falls, and it featured a steamer. It was, in fact, the first publicity stunt ever performed at Niagara Falls. The former Lake Erie steamer *Michigan* was to be dressed up as a pirate ship, with dummy people on deck, and sent to her destruction over the falls. But there was a twist. A few live creatures would be on board. When *Michigan* was ready for her ordeal, her owner loaded her with a menagerie of animals, including one buffalo, two small bears, two raccoons, a dog, one goose and maybe more.

Watched by an estimated crowd of 10,000 people, the paddle-steamer *Chippawa* towed the doomed *Michigan* out into the Niagara River. *Michigan* was turned so her bow pointed to the lip of the falls. *Chippawa*'s crew then severed the tow line and let her go. The two bears had been left loose on deck, while all the other creatures were caged, either inside or also on deck. As *Michigan* drifted close to the edge, she bumped over rocks and began to break apart. The two bears leaped overboard and were able to swim across the strong current to the sanctuary of Goat Island. The other creatures on board had no chance. They went over the falls with the wreck and were killed, except for the goose. That fortunate bird survived the 170-foot fall and was rescued from the lower river by a Mr. Duggan.

The first *Maid of the Mist* was introduced into service on the Niagara River below the falls on May 27, 1846. Far from being a tourist boat, she was there to ferry passengers across the river before the international suspension bridge was built. Once the bridge opened, the ferry service became obsolete and that early version of the now-famous *Maid of the Mist* became a sightseeing boat for tourists.

By June 1861, a significant drop in the number of passengers had put the owners of the second *Maid of the Mist* in financial jeopardy. They decided to have the boat make a dangerous run from the foot of the Horseshoe Falls through the Whirlpool Rapids to Lake Ontario where—if it survived intact—the boat would be sold. Three men were on board: Captain Joel Robinson, mechanic James McIntyre and engineer James Jones. It was a rough ride, but they made it. According to a report, "The first huge wave of the rapids threw the boat on her beam ends sending the smokestack overboard, almost submerged by the next [wave] she righted, and by a quick turn evading the whirlpool emerged from the Gorge in little over ten minutes."

Though it is unlikely that any steam-powered boats have challenged the Whirlpool Rapids since that early *Maid of the Mist*, subsequent versions of the tourist boat have carried hundreds of thousands of sightseers to the foot of Horseshoe Falls and home again. They have also been instrumental in rescuing a handful of exhibitionists who dared to go over the falls and lived to tell the tale. Today's modern *Maid of the Mist* sightseeing boats (there are actually four of them with the same name) are powered by diesel engines.

Until the late 1950s, there was a regular steamboat service between Toronto's waterfront and Niagara-on-the-Lake. Operated by SS *Cayuga*, the once-popular excursion ceased activities in the summer of 1957.

In Ontario's northern lakes and woods, the long, narrow extent of Lake Timiskaming was host to a large number of steamboats between 1881 and 1960. Effectively an extension of the Ottawa River north of Mattawa, Lake Timiskaming is 90 miles in length from Long Sault rapids (not to be confused with the rapids of the same name on the St. Lawrence River) near Témiskaming to the mouth of the des Quinze River. Steamboats also worked on Lake Nipissing and Lake Abitibi during this period, as well as on many of the rivers that linked the three lakes together. Steamboats were employed as passenger vessels, for carrying freight and as tugs to move log booms and barges.

13

The Saguenay River

NO BOOK ABOUT STEAMBOATS ON great Canadian rivers would be complete without at least a mention of the beautiful Saguenay River in Quebec. The Saguenay flows out of Lac St. Jean in the Laurentian Highlands, just west of the small communities of Naudeville and Alma. It drifts for 35 miles in an east-southeasterly direction toward Chicoutimi, where, after dropping over rapids and a steep fall, it suddenly opens up into a big river. In *Passage to the Sea*, his excellent biography of Canada Steamship Lines, Edgar Andrew Collard wrote, "Said to be the deepest in the world, flowing darkly in a chasm between abrupt and overshadowing shores, the Saguenay [River] was probably the most awesome river in Canada."

At Chicoutimi, where the Saguenay flexes its muscles and pushes the steep shores apart, the river becomes deep and takes on the aspect of a fjord. For the next 70 miles, it stretches well over one mile from shore to shore and its depth is measured in excess of 900 feet in places. Ships can steam close to the sheer walls without fear of meeting underwater obstructions. When it has finished its journey, the Saguenay empties into the St. Lawrence River on the northwest shore near Tadoussac. Today, the Saguenay River is known for its spectacular scenery and seasonal congregations of belugas and occasional minke whales.

After 1866, steam was a fixture on the Saguenay River under the auspices of the appropriately named Saguenay Line. As shipping companies go, the Saguenay Line was not a favourite with locals, but it was the only one on offer at the time. Its fleet consisted of small, old steamers that were said to be "unattractive to passengers."

In 1886, the Saguenay Line was purchased by the Richelieu and Ontario Navigation Company. The parent company's more modern and spacious ships then began serving Saguenay River towns such as Tadoussac, Bagotville and Chicoutimi (the head of navigation on that river), in addition to their regular St. Lawrence River ports. Once the newer ships became visible on the route, the passengers began filing aboard.

Passengers cruising up the fjord for Saguenay River destinations always knew when their ship reached the vicinity of L'Anse-Saint-Jean, especially at night. The ships' search-lights would play upon an immense rock until they found a particular target.

Cape Trinity is an almost sheer, massive bluff of gran-ite at the entrance to Eternity Bay. It stands over 1,300 feet high and is sparsely covered with trees. On a ledge about two-thirds of the way up is a 25-foot, white-painted pine statue of the Virgin Mary. Carved and erected in 1881 by sculptor Louis Jobin, the statue was given in gratitude to the region by Charles Robitaille, who fell through the ice but survived the freezing fjord waters by praying to the Virgin Mary.

On July 6, 1911, a brand-new ship joined the Richelieu and Ontario Navigation Company. Built on the distant Clyde for river use in Canada and named for the river she would serve, *Saguenay* was a twin-screw steamer with an interior to match any top-class hotel. The Montreal *Gazette* praised her as "one of the biggest and most perfect boats on the Canadian inland waters." Two years after she was launched, *Saguenay* joined Canada Steamship Lines when that company took over the Richelieu and Ontario Navigation Company. She served Canada Steamship Lines on the Saguenay River until she was sold in 1941.

In August 1950, SS *Quebec*, a grand-looking passen-ger ship owned by Canada Steamship Lines, caught fire in the Saguenay River. *Quebec* was built in Lauzon, Quebec, in 1928 for service between Montreal and Saguenay

River ports as a sister ship to *St. Lawrence, Richelieu* and *Tadoussac. Quebec* and *Tadoussac* were each a fraction over 7,000 tons. *St. Lawrence* was registered at 6,328 tons, and *Richelieu* was the smallest at 5,528 tons. These four ships, plus the much older and smaller *Cayuga* (used on Lake Ontario), were all that was left of the Canada Steamship Lines' once-busy passenger fleet of river and lake steamers.

Quebec was heading downriver on the Saguenay from Chicoutimi, outward bound for Montreal. She was only about four miles from Tadoussac when fire was discovered burning fiercely in a linen cupboard. It soon was out of control, and the ship, passengers and crew were in danger. Captain Cyril Birch showed his incredible navigation and piloting skills when he steered his burning ship through the swift-flowing tides and currents at the confluence of the Saguenay and St. Lawrence Rivers and delivered his charge to the Tadoussac dock. Thanks to his seamanship, 419 passengers made it safely to land, leaving only seven of their number dead on the ship. *Quebec* was not so fortunate: she burned to destruction.

The deadly fire was almost certainly caused by arson. An almost identical situation had taken place on another of the company's ships, SS *Noronic*, in Toronto harbour the year before. A fire that started in a linen cupboard destroyed the ship and took the lives of 118 persons on board. That fire was proved to be the result of arson.

In addition to the passenger steamships, the four main

Saguenay River ports (Tadoussac, La Baie, Chicoutimi and Saguenay) were also served on a regular basis by freighter traffic, much of it under the house flag of Canada Steamship Lines. Those long, lean bulk carriers were there to load cargo at the Chicoutimi pulp mills.

Today, the Saguenay River is still visited by passenger and cargo ships. They are powered by diesel engines— much less romantic than steam—but they continue the long tradition of river travel and are a colourful addition to the fjord's scenery.

CHAPTER

14

Steam on the Majestic
St. Lawrence River

THE 744 MILES OF THE St. Lawrence River stretch from the eastern end of Lake Ontario to the eastern promontory of Anticosti Island in the Gulf of St. Lawrence. During the steam era, it was the undisputed gateway to Canada from the Atlantic Ocean. Dominated by the fleets of passenger steamships operated by Canadian Pacific, the Cunard Line and Holland America Line, among others, the waterway also played host to freighters and tramps from around the world as they made their way inland to dozens of ports on the Great Lakes.

Accommodation, a side-wheel paddle-steamer built for John Molson of brewery-company fame, was the first steamboat on Canadian rivers. She began regular service between Montreal and Quebec City in 1809. The venture was not a huge financial success, but it did pave the way for the steamships of the future. Before long, Molson had a fleet of steamers carrying passengers and freight between the two major cities of the province. Molson's fleet had stiff competition, at first from the Torrance Line and later from La Compagnie du Richelieu. The ships of the three rival companies raced each other between the two St. Lawrence River ports, risking the lives of their passengers and crews as they steamed neck and neck to reach port first.

In 1830, the governments of Lower Canada and Nova Scotia introduced financial incentives to build a steamer for the Quebec City to Halifax run. That monetary carrot resulted in the Canadian-built *Royal William*, owned by a consortium of investors, including Samuel Cunard, who called themselves the Quebec and Halifax Steam Navigation Company. *Royal William* was a three-masted, schooner-rigged ship with auxiliary steam engines driving enormous side paddlewheels. She was 160 feet long and registered at 364 gross tons. Built at a Quebec City shipyard, she was towed to Montreal for the installation of her engines on the last day of April 1830.

Royal William steamed from Montreal to Quebec City on August 13. Eleven days later, she left on her first voyage to Halifax, taking six and a half days for the voyage. That time cut as much as two weeks off a sailing ship's speed. Unfortunately, what began with great fanfare died out with a whimper: *Royal William* only made that one voyage for her owners. Due to the cholera epidemic of 1832, she had to be quarantined in Halifax for much of the open-water season. By the time she was declared clean again, winter was setting in. She made an upriver voyage to Sorel and was berthed there until the spring of 1833.

In March 1833, *Royal William* was sold to six of the original investors (Samuel Cunard was not among them) for one-third of her building cost. After ice breakup, she operated a few pleasure cruises on the river and undertook occasional towing jobs. In June, the owners sent *Royal William* on a successful round-trip voyage to Boston, then decided to sell her in England. Early in August, she sailed down the St. Lawrence for the last time. Destined to enter the history books as the first ship to cross the Atlantic under steam power from west to east, she called at Pictou, Nova Scotia, and Cowes on the Isle of Wight before steaming up the Thames River to London. As far as is known, *Royal William* never returned to Canada.

As a direct consequence of the success of *Royal William*'s ocean crossing, Samuel Cunard purchased a four-year-old steamer and prepared her for a long voyage. Named *Unicorn*, she would have a significant career on the St. Lawrence River.

The brand-new Cunard steam packet *Unicorn* departed Liverpool's Clarence Dock on May 15, 1840. She was a square-rigged sailing ship with a pair of auxiliary steam engines driving a paddlewheel on either side of the hull. Built from wood on Scotland's Clyde River in 1836, *Unicorn* was 165.5 feet long, had a beam of 22.5 feet and a draft of 17.5 feet. She was registered at 903 gross tons. Honoured with the task of making the first trans-Atlantic crossing for Cunard's shipping line, she carried 453 tons of coal and 27 passengers—three for Halifax and the majority for Boston—plus she would have been staffed by up to 80 officers and crew. Captain Walter Douglas was in command. He was a veteran of the St. Lawrence River, having served there for many years as sailing master on the British surveying ship *Gulnare*. Prior to his appointment to Cunard's line, Douglas had also commanded a small steamer running between Montreal and Quebec City.

Unicorn was not intended to be an ocean-going ship. Once she had dropped her last passengers at Boston, she was scheduled to return to Halifax and then commence work in Canadian waters. The Atlantic voyage to Halifax took 16 days, with a further two days to make Boston. Captain Douglas commented that the crossing was "a very boisterous one, nothing but gales of wind from west to northwest." He added, "The 'Unicorn' is a most splendid seaboat: it blew one night a perfect hurricane, so that we could not carry our close reefed foresail. We eased the engine[s] to about half speed. Keeping the sea about a point or two points on the bow; she then went ahead about two knots as easy and dry as possible."

In her career as a mail carrier, *Unicorn* would often find similar conditions in the Gulf of St. Lawrence and on the lower reaches of the St. Lawrence River. Following her stop in Boston, *Unicorn* returned to Halifax and made a few return voyages between the two cities while waiting for the arrival from England of a larger Cunard steamer, the 1,100-ton sidewheeler *Britannia*. Once *Britannia* was in service on the Atlantic run, *Unicorn* sailed for Quebec City. From 1840 to 1844, she was employed on the St. Lawrence between Pictou, Nova Scotia, and Quebec City carrying British mail from Halifax for distribution across Canada. During that time, she was said by her captain to be "one of the best known and most important crafts on the river."

Unicorn's first arrival in sight of the Citadel overlooking Quebec was recorded in the *Quebec Mercury* newspaper:

ARRIVAL OF THE *UNICORN*.—Shortly after ten o'clock yesterday morning the repeating telegraph on Cape Diamond showed the signal for a steam vessel coming up the river . . . In about an hour from the time she was first telegraphed, this pioneer of direct steam communication between Great Britain and her North American colonies made her appearance round the point, gallantly steaming against an ebb-tide. On coming abreast of the Steamer "St. George," lying at Gibb's Wharf, a salute was fired from the "Unicorn," followed by three cheers from the people on board, which were heartily responded to from the shore.

At the end of the 1844 navigating season on the St. Lawrence, *Unicorn* left Quebec for the last time and sailed for Halifax, where she spent the winter. She was later employed on charters from New York to the West Indies and ended her working life as a Portuguese gunboat.

Winter ice was a major drawback to shipping on the St. Lawrence River. At best, the navigation season extended from April to December. In 1840, the Port of Montreal commissioners offered a symbolic award for the first ocean-going ship to reach Montreal at the beginning of each season. The original award was a top hat. Forty years later, that was upgraded to the gold-headed cane that has been awarded annually ever since.

On May 15, 1853, a British sailing steamer, *Genova*, docked at Montreal. She was intended to offer regular sailings carrying passengers and mail between Liverpool and Montreal, but the service failed soon after it started. *Genova* made just the one voyage before fading into obscurity.

Over the next 50 years or so, freight traffic between European ports and Montreal kept the St. Lawrence busy with steamer traffic. The number of passenger liners on the river also increased, with the ships becoming larger.

The loss of ships at sea had been a potential hazard of ocean travel since the first sailing ships ventured away from land. Few, however, would have predicted a major maritime disaster on a river, although the rapidly growing number of ships serving the St. Lawrence River in the 19th century and early years of the 20th century might have given reason to fear this possibility.

In 1842, the steamer *Shamrock* was outbound upriver from Montreal for Kingston. While transiting the Lachine Canal, *Shamrock*'s boiler exploded, killing 54 out of the 120 passengers and crew on board. Close to the end of June 1857, SS *Montreal* left Quebec City for Montreal carrying an estimated 500 passengers. An hour or so into the voyage, *Montreal* caught fire. Two other steamers in the vicinity, *Napoleon* and *Alliance*, altered course to assist. Captain Rudolph of *Montreal* stopped his ship and was preparing to run her ashore when it became obvious that the fire had taken too strong a hold. Those who could swim dived overboard, and many were rescued by the two steamers standing by. Over 300 people died because of the fire.

Disasters due to fire were infrequent, but there was another potential danger lurking on the river: too many ships and not enough controls. In truth, a collision between two ships in the relatively narrow waterway was inevitable. In May 1914, the St. Lawrence River was the scene of a tragic marine accident that caused 1,012 deaths, a disaster comparable to the sinking of *Titanic* with the loss of 1,517 people just two years before. The Canadian Pacific ship RMS *Empress of Ireland* was outbound from Quebec City en route for Liverpool when her planned course down the St. Lawrence and across the North Atlantic was abruptly terminated only a few hours into the voyage. The sleek

Empress of Ireland left Quebec City at 16:30 local time on Thursday, May 28, 1914, for her 96th ocean crossing. On board were 1,057 passengers in three classes, plus 420 officers and crew. *Empress* was 570 feet long and registered at 14,191 gross tons.

The St. Lawrence River pilot had been dropped at Father Point, near Rimouski, and the ship was steaming down the correct channel. Her next stop should have been in an English port. In the early hours of May 29, Captain Kendall was on the bridge. He identified lights off the starboard bow as those of an approaching ship and altered course to avoid her. Although Kendall didn't know it at the time, the lights belonged to the much smaller Norwegian collier *Storstad*, heading upriver from Sydney, Nova Scotia.

The St. Lawrence River is known for its sudden fogs, and that May night was no exception. *Storstad* was swallowed up by a fog, and Kendall had no idea where she was. He took evasive action, ringing down to his engine room for "full astern" to slow his ship and put her in reverse. At the same time, he signalled his intentions with three blasts from *Empress*'s steam whistle. There was no answer from the collier, still hidden in the fog. Kendall stopped the ship and sounded two more shrieking whistle blasts. A few minutes later, at five minutes before two in the morning *Storstad* emerged from the fog on a collision course with the passenger liner. Kendall called down for "full steam ahead" to avoid the collier, but it was too late. *Storstad*'s bow slammed into *Empress* on her starboard side and gouged a 350-foot-long hole. The collier slid along the liner's hull and continued on her way in the fog.

The stricken ship, with water pouring into her engine room, was two miles from the nearest land. Kendall rang down for every whisper of steam, hoping to beach the *Empress* in shallow water. The damage, however, was far too great. While passengers and some off-duty crew slept, she went down in 140 feet of water, only 14 minutes after the collision.

SOS calls had radiated out from her wireless room and had been heard. *Storstad*, having caused the accident, turned back and rescued some of the survivors. Meanwhile, two other steamers, *Eureka* and *Lady Evelyn*, were not far away at Father Point, and they had steam up and were ready for sea. They cast off their moorings and hurried to the desperate scene. Between them, they rescued hundreds of additional passengers and crew struggling in the water.

At this time, the First World War was imminent. In fact, it started in Europe exactly one month after the collision between the two ships on the other side of the Atlantic. As a sad result, the tragic story of the passengers and crew of RMS *Empress of Ireland* was swept off the front pages of the world's newspapers and replaced with more immediate news. Today the remains of *Empress of Ireland* rest in peace as a national historic site, with the hull lying undisturbed on its starboard side, exactly where it fell that long-ago night.

Despite the occasional tragic accident, steamships were a popular means of transporting passengers and freight. A Canadian company, Canada Steamship Lines, the end result of a series of steamship company acquisitions and mergers, owned the largest inland fleet of steamships in the world at the time. After the Second World War ended in November 1945, Canada Steamship Lines commissioned a series of new passenger-carrying steamships. Added to the existing inventory, collectively they became known as the "Great White Fleet." The steamships varied in size and purpose. The three largest were for travel on the Great Lakes, while the others were placed where they were needed. Each stage of the inland river voyage from the mouth of the St. Lawrence River to the Great Lakes required a different ship. Three Canada Steamship Line ships ran the section of the St. Lawrence that involved navigating the Long Sault and Lachine Rapids. They ranged from the old *Rapids Queen*, built in 1892, to the reliable *Rapids Prince* and the unstable *Rapids King*, which was said to roll abominably.

Running the two sets of rapids on the St. Lawrence River between Kingston and Montreal required extremely skilled pilots. The Long Sault Rapids was a long, steady descent over nine miles of whitewater. The rapids were noisy, and running them in a ship was a thrilling experience, but it was nothing compared to the next adventure; farther downstream, on the outskirts of Montreal, the Lachine Rapids waited. Edgar Andrew Collard described the descent

Passenger steamers such as Canada Steamship Lines's *Rapids Queen* regularly navigated up and down the difficult Lachine Rapids on the St. Lawrence River in the late 19th and early 20th centuries.
LIBRARY AND ARCHIVES CANADA C-022153

Passage to the Sea: "The real thrill came from dodging huge rocks. Many were half submerged ... Again and again the ship seemed to rush at a rock, as though out of control. When the rock was only seconds away the pilot whirled the wheel ... The ship swerved with a jolt and swept by the rock."

The original Lachine Canal was completed in 1825, but it was too shallow for steamboats. The locks and canal were enlarged between 1843 and 1848 and again between 1873 and 1885. Once the canal was ready, ships could travel that section of the river in safety, but without the attendant thrills of nearby whitewater.

In 1950, the 26,313-ton *Empress of Scotland* became the largest steamship to navigate up the St. Lawrence River all the way to Montreal. The author travelled on her from Liverpool to Montreal in October 1957. www.PHOTOSHIP.CO.UK

In 1950, after an extensive refit at Liverpool, the 26,313-ton SS *Empress of Scotland*, flagship of the Canadian Pacific fleet, began seven years of trans-Atlantic crossings from Liverpool to Montreal, via Greenock on the Clyde and Quebec City. During the refit, her two masts had been shortened to allow her to steam under the Jacques Cartier Bridge to reach her dock at Montreal. When she tied up at the end of that first 1950 voyage, she became the largest ship to navigate the St. Lawrence all the way to Montreal.

By the mid-1950s, Canadian Pacific was positioned

to have four passenger-carrying *Empresses* on the North Atlantic route from Liverpool to Montreal. The two older ships, *Empress of France* and *Empress of Scotland*, were joined in 1956 by *Empress of Britain* and *Empress of England* and in 1960 by the new *Empress of Canada*. Meanwhile, in the first half of the 1950s, the Cunard Line also had a substantial fleet of four ships serving the route: *Ivernia*, *Saxonia*, *Carinthia* and *Sylvania*; and Holland America Line operated the smaller *Ryndam*.

Suddenly there were too many ships and not enough passengers. During the later years of the 1950s and into the 1960s, there was a rapid decline in steamship travel for passengers across the Atlantic. International air travel was increasing in popularity and taking a heavy toll on its much slower seaborne competitors. By the mid-1960s, the steam era was over. A few passenger ships still made regular voyages up and down the St. Lawrence, among them the recently launched *Empress of Canada*. By this time, the cargo vessels on the route had all been converted to diesel power. A magnificent epoch had come to an end.

Epilogue

STEAM WAS NEVER A PARTICULARLY efficient means of propelling a large vessel, and the fuel required came at significant cost to those who dug it out of mines deep underground or chopped it out of the forests. In the early years, enormous amounts of expensive coal had to be carried to feed the voracious boilers on seagoing ships. Trimmers and firemen, often known as the "black gang," worked deep in the bowels of steamships. Without their extraordinary efforts at very low pay, the ships' fires could never have produced steam in the boilers. Firemen, also called stokers, fed the fires and controlled their heat. Trimmers had the unenviable task of keeping piles of coal at hand for the stokers, as well as removing buckets of hot ash when required.

Epilogue

On the interior rivers of Canada, the steamers, which could burn wet wood as well as dry, consumed millions of trees that had been cut into cordwood, as well as any driftwood found and occasional abandoned wooden shacks. In fact, if the need was there, any combustible item would do to get the boat to the nearest stand of trees or its destination.

Apart from a few historic coal- or oil-fired steamers still operating in the 21st century in places such as Scandinavia and New Zealand, the much more efficient diesel engine had become the power plant of choice for ships by the 1960s. The introduction of diesel-powered vessels eliminated the need for coal or wood as fuels.

The advent of mass air travel in the late 1950s and early 1960s reduced and soon eliminated the need for ships as passenger carriers. Cargo, either in containers or in bulk, is still carried across the world's oceans but, with the exception of cruise ships, the romance of crossing oceans in passenger liners has gone the way of the steam engine.

Selected Bibliography

Affleck, Edward L. *A Century of Paddlewheelers in the Pacific Northwest, the Yukon and Alaska*. Vancouver: Alexander Nicholls Press, 2000.

Backhouse, Frances. *Children of the Klondike*. Vancouver: Whitecap, 2010.

Barris, Theodore. *Fire Canoe: Prairie Steamboat Days Revisited*. Toronto: McClelland and Stewart, 1977.

Berton, Pierre. *Klondike: The Last Great Gold Rush, 1896–1899*. Rev. ed. Toronto: McClelland and Stewart, 1978.

Blower, James. *Gold Rush*. Toronto: McGraw-Hill, 1971.

Bocking, Richard C. *Mighty River: A Portrait of the Fraser*. Vancouver: Douglas & McIntyre, 1997.

Boudreau, Jack. *Sternwheelers and Canyon Cats*. Madeira Park, BC: Caitlin Press, 2006.

Boyden, Joseph. *Louis Riel & Gabriel Dumont*. Toronto: Penguin, 2010.

Collard, Edgar Andrew. *Passage to the Sea: The Story of Canada Steamship Lines*. Toronto: Doubleday, 1991.

Cumberland, Barlow. *A Century of Sail and Steam on the Niagara River*. Toronto: Musson Books, 1913.

Dalrymple, A.J. "'Cap' Ross of the Saskatchewan." *The Beaver* (June 1944): 20–23.

Dalton, Anthony. *The Fur-Trade Fleet*. Victoria: Heritage House, 2011.

Douglas, James Jr. "The Steamship Unicorn." Literary and Historical Society of Quebec *Transactions*, New Series, no. 28 (1910).

Selected Bibliography

Galbraith, William. "Lord Tweedsmuir's Visit to the North: Never Be off the Road." *Canadian Parliamentary Review* 18, no. 1 (1995).

Gray, Charlotte. *Gold Diggers*. Toronto: HarperCollins, 2010.

Jones, David Laurence. *Tales of the CPR*. Calgary: Fifth House, 2002.

Langley, John G. *Steam Lion: A Biography of Samuel Cunard*. Halifax: Nimbus, 2006.

Legget, Robert. *Ottawa Waterway*. Toronto: University of Toronto Press, 1975.

MacGregor, James Grierson. *Paddle Wheels to Bucket Wheels on the Athabasca*. Toronto: McClelland and Stewart, 1974.

McFadden, Molly. "Steamboats to the Rescue, 1897." *Manitoba Pageant* 6, no. 3 (April 1961).

Newman, Peter C. *Merchant Princes*. Toronto: Viking, 1991.

Pigott, Peter. *Sailing Seven Seas: A History of the Canadian Pacific Line*. Toronto: Dundurn Press, 2010.

Stefansson, Vilhjalmur. *My Life with the Eskimo*. New York: Macmillan, 1913.

Tatley, Richard. *Northern Steamboats*. Erin, ON: Boston Mills Press, 1998.

Taylor, R.J. "Captain Ross—Laird of the River." *Manitoba Pageant* 3, no. 2 (January 1958).

Turner, Robert D. *Sternwheelers and Steam Tugs*. Winlaw, BC: Sono Nis Press, 1984.

———. *The S.S. Moyie: Memories of the Oldest Sternwheeler*. Victoria: Sono Nis Press, 1991.

Index

Index

Acknowledgements

Ships and boats of all sizes and descriptions have been a passion of mine since I was a boy. I built my first boat from abandoned 45-gallon oil drums and some old rope. At the age of about eight, I paddled that strange and unsafe craft around a flooded gravel quarry near Oxford, England, until it disintegrated—with me on board. Decades later, I paddled an equally primitive, but much safer dugout canoe across Africa's Okavango River to reach Angola. In between, I have crossed the North Atlantic on passenger liners, and I have sailed that same great ocean, as well as other seas, as a crew member on tall ships. I have cruised on sailboats and helped deliver expensive motor yachts; I have driven small motorboats in extreme conditions, rowed traditional boats and paddled canoes. I have enjoyed them all, and I thank the owners and crews of the bigger boats and ships for the opportunities they gave me.

Without the staff at Heritage House my writing career would possibly not be as much fun as it has become. I feel that I am part of a large and wonderful family. Again, my sincere thanks and appreciation go to publisher Rodger Touchie, managing editor Vivian Sinclair, editor Lesley Reynolds, proofreaders Karla Decker and Liesbeth Leatherbarrow, production manager Susan Adamson, designers Chyla Cardinal, Francis Hunter and Jacqui Thomas, marketing specialist Neil Wedin, all the sales representatives, and the friendly and efficient staff at the distribution centre in Surrey. You have my admiration for your cheerful professionalism.

I must thank underwater archaeologist and fellow explorer John Pollack for sharing his knowledge of the old steamers from western and northern Canada. Steve Crowhurst gets a mention in almost all my books, and he deserves it. Without his influence I might never have become a writer. Thanks old pal: I owe you so much. Thanks also to long-time friend and fellow writer, JayBee, for much encouragement. Finally, my appreciation for ongoing support and advice goes to my friend Bernice Lever.

About the Author

Anthony Dalton is the author of 11 non-fiction books and co-author of two others, many of which are about the sea, ships or adventures in a variety of boats. These include *The Fur-Trade Fleet; Polar Bears; A Long, Dangerous Coastline; The Graveyard of the Pacific; Baychimo: Arctic Ghost Ship;* and *Alone Against the Arctic,* all published by Heritage House. He is past president of the Canadian Authors Association and is dedicated to the craft of writing. Since the fall of 2011, Anthony has been travelling the world as a featured guest speaker on a variety of cruise ships for two cruise lines. He is a former expedition leader working in the Sahara, the deserts of the Middle East and occasionally in the Arctic. When at home in British Columbia, he divides his time between Tsawwassen and the nearby Gulf Islands.

More Amazing Stories by Anthony Dalton

Polar Bears
The Arctic's Fearless Great Wanderers

print ISBN 978-1-926613-74-1
ebook ISBN 978-1-926936-25-3

Polar bears have become a charismatic symbol of animals threatened by climate change, yet in the past they were feared and hunted indiscriminately by Arctic adventurers. These fascinating stories draw from the annals of northern exploration and more recent polar bear research to capture the power and majesty of the world's largest land carnivore.

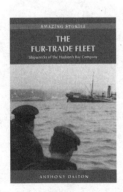

The Fur-Trade Fleet
Shipwrecks of the Hudson's Bay Company

print ISBN 978-1-926936-09-3
ebook ISBN 978-1-926936-07-9

Since the 17th century, hundreds of ships have sailed in the Hudson's Bay Company's fur-trade fleet, servicing far-flung northern posts and braving the wild rapids of mighty rivers. During these arduous voyages, many of these ships and their courageous crews came to grief. Here are the dramatic stories of the legendary ships that proudly flew the flag of Canada's oldest company.

Visit heritagehouse.ca to see the entire list of books in this series.

More Amazing Stories by Anthony Dalton

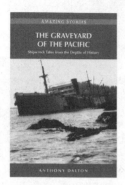

The Graveyard of the Pacific
Shipwreck Tales from the Depths of History

print ISBN 978-1-926613-31-4
ebook ISBN 978-1-926936-31-4

The magnificent west coast of Vancouver Island is renowned for its rugged splendour, but the coastline known as the Graveyard of the Pacific is haunted by the ghosts of doomed ships and long-dead mariners. These true tales of disastrous shipwrecks and daring rescues are a fascinating adventure into West Coast maritime history.

A Long, Dangerous Coastline
Shipwreck Tales from Alaska to California

print ISBN 978-1-926613-73-4
ebook ISBN 978-1-926936-11-6

From San Francisco's Golden Gate to the Inside Passage of British Columbia and Alaska, the west coast of North America has taken a deadly toll. Here are the dramatic tales of ships that met their end on this treacherous coastline—including *Princess Sophia*, *Queen of the North* and others—and the tragic stories of those who sailed aboard them.

Visit heritagehouse.ca to see the entire list of books in this series.